COLLECTOR'S HANDBOOK TO MARKS ON PORCELAIN AND POTTERY

Edited by
E. PAUL and A. PETERSEN

MODERN BOOKS AND CRAFTS, INC.
GREENS FARMS, CONN. 06436 U.S.A.

Printed in the United States of America

INTRODUCTION

THE ardent collector of Pottery or Porcelain, even when he has long passed his "novitiate," constantly feels the need of a reliable pocket volume containing the authentic and indisputable marks of the pottery and porcelain of the best "collectors'" periods. It has been our aim to supply such a volume in a condensed and practical form. The only marks given in this book are those which are beyond dispute. The arrangement is geographical, the different species of ware being separately treated wherever practicable ; but, by elaborate indices, ready reference has been provided to each mark, as well as to each factory. In addition, a condensed account of the important productions of every country prefaces each section of the work. The aim, throughout, has been to render the work as complete and self-contained as such a pocket manual can be ; though, in his study, the collector will naturally turn for fuller information to the important histories or monographs, such as those mentioned in the bibliography.

It has been assumed that the collector is acquainted with the broad distinctions of Simple Pottery, Faïence, Stoneware, and Porcelain. The terms are used here in a very definite way.

> SIMPLE POTTERY includes all the forms of earthenware whether made from white or coloured clays, glazed with a transparent lead glaze.
>
> FAÏENCE includes all the forms of earthenware, coated with tin-enamel, such as Majolica, Delft, and their related types.

STONEWARE includes the hard, vitrified and impermeable kinds of earthenware, whether Rhenish, English, or Oriental.

PORCELAINS are the translucent and (generally) white forms of pottery.

The porcelains are classified in the customary way, as hard-paste or soft-paste. The hard-paste group includes such well-defined types as the Chinese, Japanese, German, and modern Continental porcelains. The soft-paste group includes all the porcelains in which the fired body is distinctly softer than in the former group. The soft-paste porcelains comprise two distinct varieties, which are of widely different value to the collector.

A. The soft-paste glassy porcelains (invaluable on account of their quality and rarity), such as those made at Florence (sixteenth century), Rouen (seventeenth century), and the early French and English porcelains (eighteenth century);

B. The soft bone-paste porcelains, such as the English porcelains made in the later eighteenth and throughout the nineteenth century.

So much attention has been paid to marks that it may be necessary to state clearly the exact value of a mark. Other things being equal, a marked example of any period is more valuable than an unmarked one. But the mark alone must not be considered as the sole criterion of excellence or even market value. Unfortunately since factory or workmen's marks have become general, quite a large proportion of pieces have been sent out without any distinctive mark, especially in byegone centuries. This has been the opportunity of the forger and "faker," and the reader is earnestly warned to be on his guard against their abominable cleverness. The marks which are most difficult to imitate, and are in that respect most reliable, are those which occur under the glaze; as was generally the case before the eighteenth century. During the eighteenth century there was a gradual introduction of marks painted, printed, or stencilled over the glaze, and this practice has been increasingly followed, with some exceptions, to the present day.

The under-glaze marks are of two kinds : (*a*) those stamped or incised in the body of the ware while it is still soft. These are perhaps the most reliable of all marks, for once made it is very difficult to remove or alter them. They may, however, be so imperfectly formed, or have been so obliterated by the glaze as to be deciphered with difficulty. (*b*) Marks painted under the glaze. This is the most important class of marks, being found on Oriental porcelain, Persian earthenware, European faïence, and nearly every kind of European pottery and porcelain. Down to the end of the eighteenth century, practically all under-glaze marks were in blue (the most available colour), and it is only in the nineteenth century, as a rule, that under-glaze marks in black, pink, or green are found. Many of these later marks are printed and not painted. In all the old wares, where not otherwise specified, it may be taken for granted that the mark is painted in blue.

With the introduction of over-glaze, or enamel, colours and gilding in the eighteenth century we get an increasing use of marks in the same style. The fact that these marks are painted over the glaze detracts greatly from their value, for several reasons. Such marks are easily added to any piece of pottery or porcelain, as they can be fired at a temperature that will not seriously impair the previous decoration. Genuine over-glaze marks can be readily removed and a more valuable mark substituted, so that they cannot be regarded in themselves as being so safe and trustworthy as those which occur under the glaze.

The marks themselves consist of factory names, or trade-marks as they are called nowadays, the signatures of potters, painters, or gilders, with or without dates and descriptive notes, placed in some inconspicuous place, occasionally in the design, but generally under the base of the piece. Some of them, especially the early ones, afford precise information as to the origin of the piece on which they occur, but others are mere workmen's signs or pattern marks, or numbers which are of little value unless supported by other evidence. The tendency of many old factories (and some modern ones) to borrow each other's marks, or to adopt signs similar to those in use at some more famous works, is a source of endless confusion which can only be avoided by a knowledge of the wares themselves.

The period covered extends roughly from the Middle Ages to 1850, though a selection of certain modern marks has been included, especially of such wares as are already finding favour with collectors. No attempt has been made to reproduce the exact size of the individual marks, because of the constant variations in size and form of the same painted mark on different pieces. Stamped and written names have been reproduced in Roman and Italic types respectively, except in those cases where striking individuality of script rendered a direct copy necessary. Each new factory, or group of factories, as it occurs is printed in conspicuous type. The dates given for the European wares require no explanation, but in the Oriental sections, with which especial pains have been taken, the dates are those of the actual specimen from which the mark was copied. These Oriental marks cannot be regarded as date-marks when they are mere symbols or benevolent expressions.

CONTENTS

POTTERY MARKS

ABBREVIATIONS USED IN THIS WORK.

h.p. = hard-paste porcelain.

s.p. = soft-paste porcelain.

p. = painted.

pr. = printed.

inc. = incised.

imp. = impressed or stamped.

st. = stencilled.

WORKS OF REFERENCE CONSULTED

Auscher, E. S., A History and Description of French Porcelain.

Barber, E. A., Marks of American Potters.

Berling, F., Das Meissner Porzellan und seine Geschichte.

Brinckmann, J., Führer durch das hamburgisches Museum für Kunst und Gewerbe.

Burton, W., A History and Description of English Porcelain.

A History and Description of English Earthenware and Stoneware.

Chaffers, W., Marks and Monograms on Pottery and Porcelain.

Church, A. H., The Catalogue of the Schreiber Collection.

English Earthenware.

English Porcelain.

In series of Victoria and Albert Museum Handbooks.

Fortnum, C. D., Maiolica.

Fouquet, D., Contribution à l'étude de la céramique orientale.

Franks, Sir A. W., Catalogue of a Collection of Continental Porcelain at the Bethnal Green Museum.

Catalogue of a Collection of Oriental Porcelain and Pottery.

Japanese Pottery.

Graesse-Zimmermann, Führer für Sammler, etc.

Havard, H., La Faïence de Delft.

Hayden, A., Royal Copenhagen Porcelain.

Hobson, R. L., The Catalogue of English Pottery in the British Museum.

The Catalogue of English Porcelain in the British Museum.

Chinese Pottery and Porcelain.

Hofmann, Fr., Das europäische Porzellan des Bayerischen National Museum.

Jaennicke, F., Grundriss der Keramik.

Jewitt, Ll., The Ceramic Art of Great Britain.

Justice, J., Marques et monogrammes de la faïence de Delft.

Morse, Prof. E. S., Catalogue of Japanese Pottery in the Museum of Fine Arts. Boston, U.S.A.

Riesebieter, O., Die deutschen Fayencen.

Solon, L. M., German Stoneware.

A History and Description of the Old French Faience.

Von Falke, O., Das rheinische Steinzeug.

ITALIAN MAIOLICA

THE term MAIOLICA is applied in these pages to the decorated Italian pottery made from the fifteenth century onwards, though it is often used to embrace certain kinds of ware to which the name is not strictly applicable, viz. mezza-maiolica, *graffiato* wares, and the later lead-glazed, white earthenwares of the eighteenth and nineteenth centuries.

MEZZA-MAIOLICA is the name given to a common buff earthenware, coated with a wash of white clay (slip), and painted in simple, often crude tints of green, blue, and purplish brown, under a thin colourless glaze. It was the precursor of true maiolica.

GRAFFIATO ware is a mezza-maiolica, with a substantial coating of white slip, which was decorated by scratching or cutting out a pattern through this slip-covering, so as to disclose the buff or red body beneath—colours, if used at all, were usually added in patches or washes—and in any case the ware was finished with a clear, straw-coloured, lead glaze. This, like the painted mezza-maiolica, was a very early type of product, which, however, has continued in use, in the north of Italy especially, to the present time.

MAIOLICA proper was fashioned in a buff ware, more carefully prepared and closer in texture than mezza-maiolica, and is coated with a white, opaque layer of tin-enamel (instead of slip), on which the painter laid his colours : the later and more delicately painted maiolica was finished with an additional thin coat of colourless glaze, applied over the fired colours, like the varnish over a picture. Up to the eighteenth century one firing sufficed for the colours and the tin-enamel, and only such pigments could be used as would stand the full heat of the maiolica kiln. The marks, on wares of this period, are almost always in blue.

Early in the eighteenth century a new process was introduced. The body and its tin-enamel coating were baked and finished first, then the decoration was applied to the fired surface in on-the-glaze colours, which were fixed at a comparatively low heat in the enamelling kiln. From this time marks in various colours on the glaze became common.

The most famous period of true maiolica was from about 1500 to 1560 when the typical decoration consisted of pictorial subjects copied from engravings after the great Italian painters. The marks at this period are often very elaborate, and tell us not only the name of the painter of the piece, but the botega or factory in which he worked, the name of the master under whom he served, and the title of his subject. Hence the frequent occurrence of such words (sometimes in contracted form) as botega, maestro, vasaro (potter), pictor, fatto (made), fecit, pinxit, etc. On the lustred wares of Diruta and Gubbio the mark is usually in lustre. Maestro Giorgio Andreoli of Gubbio (*q.v.*) was famed for his skill in the production of lustres, especially ruby lustre, and the potters of other towns sometimes sent their pieces to Gubbio, after they had been painted and fired, to be embellished with lustre by Giorgio. Such pieces bear Giorgio's mark in lustre, in addition to the mark or signature of the original painter, which is in blue.

ITALIAN PORCELAIN

THE earliest European porcelain, of which marked examples are known, was made at Florence under the patronage of Francesco Maria di Medici in the last half of the sixteenth century, and is called "Medici Porcelain." This "Medici" porcelain owed its translucence to the glass used in its preparation. It is among the rarest of ceramic treasures, and an authentic specimen is worth many times its weight in gold. Little more is heard of Italian porcelain until about the middle of the eighteenth century, when the rage for porcelain manufacture was at its height in Europe.

Hard porcelain in imitation of the celebrated Meissen porcelain, as well as soft-paste porcelain, was then made at Venice successively by Vezzi, Hewelcke, and the Cozzi family. The more famous porcelain made at Doccia (1737 onwards) was a soft paste during the early years of the factory, but a hard paste was made afterwards, and the same may be said of the royal factory, started at Capo di Monte in 1743, and subsequently transferred to Naples. At Treviso and Vinovo another kind of porcelain, containing silicate of magnesia, was produced for a few years at the end of the eighteenth century. This ware has a yellowish waxen appearance which is peculiar to certain Italian and Spanish factories.

Mark.	Description.	Mark.	Description.
	Graffiato Ware Citta di Castello or Perugia c. 1520		Caffaggiolo or Faenza c. 1500
G.F.F. 1560 PI GIVLIE A SFORZZA			,, c. 1510
M. F.	c. 1650		
IOHANNES. ANTONIUS. BARNABAS. CUTIUS. PAPIÆNSIS	1676 and other members of the Cuzio family at Pavia		,, ,,
			,, c. 1510-20 (Monogram of P.L.A.T.)
1734 *la 26 marzo* Pavia			
	Maiolica proper. **Tuscany**		,, 1515-20
	Caffaggiolo or Florence 1491		,, 1500-20
	Florence 15th cent.		? Caffaggiolo 1507
	Caffaggiolo c. 1500		Caffaggiolo
	Caffaggiolo ,,		? ,,
	Faenza c. 1500		,, 1500-20

MARK.	DESCRIPTION.	MARK.	DESCRIPTION.
	Caffaggiolo c. 1520 1513 1513-21		**Caffaggiolo** c. 1550 In Galiano, a hamlet near Caffaggiolo
fata ī Siena da mº benedetto	in a panel on which is a cupid c. 1520		The Rape of Helen, made in Monte (a hamlet near Caffaggiolo) **Siena** Maestro Benedetto c. 1510-20 c. 1510

MARK.	DESCRIPTION.	MARK.	DESCRIPTION.
Ferdinando Maria Campani Senese dipinse 1733.	**Siena**	C·H·O·N	**Pesaro** c. 1510
	? F. Campani.		
PISA	**Pisa** 16th century		1500-10 (Pessaro or Faenza)
RAFAELLO GIROLAMO FECIT MTE. LUPO 1639	**Montelupo**		? Pesaro
Dipinta Giovinale Tereni da Montelupo			,,
F. P. Asciani	**Asciano** 1600		,,
F. F. D. FORTUNATUS PHILLIGELLUS P. ASCIANI	1578	*in la botega da mastro Girolamo da le Gabice* *In Pesaro*	1542 Made in the Lanfranchi workshop by Mo. Girolamo (or Gironimo)
	Pesaro Early 16th cent.	*Fato in botega di Mastro Gironimo Vasaro I. P.*	I. P. = Jacomo pinxit, Jacomo was son of Girolamo
	1520-30	*Terencio fecit in la bottega di Mastro Baldessar Vasaro da Pesaro*	1550

MARK.	DESCRIPTION.	MARK.	DESCRIPTION.
1548 *di Maestro T.*	**Pesaro** Terencio		**Gubbio** Giorgio's mark is sometimes accompanied by a head, a vase, a merchant's mark, etc.
I. S.			
C.:C. pesaro 1765 Pi:p:L:̇	Casali and Caligari, painted by Pietro Lei		
	? Francesco de' Fattori 18th cent.		
F. F.			
	Gubbio		
	1490-1500 ? Gubbio		
	? Gubbio		? Salimbene, brother of Giorgio
			,, c. 1530
			N is supposed to contain the letters V I N, and to be the monogram of Vincencio, son of Giorgio
	c. 1525 Marks of Maestro Giorgio Andreoli whose dated works range from 1501-41		Other initials, *e.g.* D, M, occur in Gubbio lustre

MARK.	DESCRIPTION.	MARK.	DESCRIPTION.
			Castel Durante
	Pesaro or Gubbio c. 1480	*kk*	c. 1520
	? G. A. for Giorgio Andreoli c. 1540	*1526 jn caſtel Durante*	
	Probably for Mº Giorgio	*·S·B·*	
		IN TERR(A) DVRANTIS	
In gŭbio ꝑ. mano đ maſtro preſtino	Prestino fl. 1536-57		1532
	,,		
	Carocci, Fabbri, & Co. 19th cent.		
		P. Mastro Simono in Castelo Durate	1562
		S.	1580
	Castel Durante.	G. S.	c. 1530
		F. R.	
facta fu ī Castel duratⁱ zonā maria vrō	Giovanni Maria, potter 1508		
		H. R.	in scrolls
Ne la botega đ Sebastiano đ Marforio	1519	*Hipollito Rombaldoni d Urbania pinse 1647*	Urbania = Castel Durante

MARK.	DESCRIPTION.	MARK.	DESCRIPTION.
	Urbino		**Urbino**
	monograms of Nicola Pellipario, also called Nicola da Urbino, who came to Urbino in 1519 and worked in the botega of his son Guido Fontana. He died about 1550		Orazio Fontana
			? Orazio Fontana
		FATTO IN BOTEGA DE M⁰ ORATO FONTANA	
			Flaminio Fontana 1583
		SFORZA. D. P.	1567
	1528	*frā Xanto. A. da Rovigo ī Urbino pī*	Francesco Xanto Avelli da Rovigo whose signed works range from 1530-42
fatte in Urbino in botega de M⁰ Guido fontana vasaro	Fontana family		
nella botega de M⁰ Guido durantino in Urbino. 1535			
L.V.	on a dish attributed to Orazio Fontana		The words, *historia*, *nota*, or *fabula*, and a description of the subjects occur on pieces painted by a pupil of Xanto
	Monograms of Orazio Fontana fl. 1540-71	F.X.A.R. *piltor*	
		historia	
		nota	
		frācesco durantino	Francesco Durantino c. 1544

MARK.	DESCRIPTION.	MARK.	DESCRIPTION.
	Urbino		**Urbino**
Francesco Durātino Vasaro A mōte Bagnolo d̄ Peroscia	1553 Probably at Bagnara, a village near Perugia	1549 ⚬ ƉG	? Caesari Cari 1536-51
In Urbino nella botteg di Francesco de Si Luano	1541 =Silvano	SAM	? Simone di Antonio Mariani
fato in Botega de Guido Merlino	1551	GBF	1630 uncertain
Gironimo Urbin fecie 1583		*Puerras* ·F·G·	1654 ,,
gironimo et tomaso	1575		
FGC	in scrolls c. 1580	*Pompio* O. F. V 1590	
2 M P S	by the same artist 1542 uncertain	G. L. P	1667 ,,
GOBO	1531 ,,	*Urbini Patana fecit*	1584 The Patanazzi family
ℒC		ALFONSO PATANAZZI FECIT URBIN	1606
ℒ	,,		
☽	,,	URBINI EX FIGLINA FRANCISCI PATANATII	1608
♆	with initials and date EFB 1594	*vincentio patanatai de anni 12*	by Vincenzio at the age of 12 in 1619
·O·A· P·P ·1548·	c. 1540	E. B.	School of the Patanazzi

MARK.	DESCRIPTION.	MARK.	DESCRIPTION.
Fabrica di Maiolica fina di Monsiur Rolet in Urbino . . . 1773	**Urbino**		**Diruta**
Citta Borgo S. Sepolcro Mart. Roletus fecit	at **Borgo San Sepolcro** 1771		
Bar Terchi Romano in S. Quirico	**San Quirico D'Orcia** Bartolomeo Terchi worked also at Bassano (*q.v.*)		with the words IN DERVTA 1544
Bar : Terc Romano		deruta çe el fiun. pemse	El Frate pinse (= painted it)
	Diruta		
I·DERVTA G.	1505		
	1480	Incleruta Srate fecit	1545
	in a shield c. 1530		
	Early Diruta		
franco. Urbini i deruta	1537	G. V. *Antonio Lafreri In Deruta*	Probably Giorgio Vasaio 1554

MARK.	DESCRIPTION.	MARK.	DESCRIPTION.
1771 FABRICA DI MAIOLICA FINA DI GREGORIO CAS ELLI IN DI RUTA	**Diruta**	IO SILVESTRO D'AGELO TRINCI DA DERVTA FATTᵒ IN BAGNIOREA 1691	? in village of Bagnara (see p. 10)
C B			
℞	? Diruta	*fabriano* 1527	Fabriano
CDL			
B	with lustred scrolls		
	c. 1560 ? Diruta		
1544	,,	IFR VITERBIEN	Viterbo
	,,	IN VITERBO 1544	on a ribbon

MARK.	DESCRIPTION.	MARK.	DESCRIPTION.
1579 *fato in botega da Antonio da Casteldurate in Roma*	**Rome**		**Faenza**
			15th century marks
FATTO IN BOTEGA DE M. DIOMEDE DURANTE IN ROMA	1600		
FATTO IN ROMA DA GĪO PAULO SAVĪNO			Faenza or Florence 1460
ALMA ROMA 1623			Faenza or Caffaggiolo 1490
D⸱M ROMA MAG⸱1769			On pavement tiles in the Church of San Sebastiano, Venice, 1510.
G⸱VOLPATO⸱ROMA	on porcelain biscuit and white pottery figures 1790-1831		Faenza 1510-20
PETRUS ANDREA DE FA BOLOGNI BETINI FEC 1487	**Faenza** Signatures on pavement tiles at Bologna in the San Petronio		? Betini family others assign these marks to Castel Durante

MARK.	DESCRIPTION.	MARK.	DESCRIPTION.
	Faenza		**Faenza**
	Initials of a pharmacy		Casa Pirota c. 1525
			c. 1525
	c. 1520		
			1531
	The Casa Pirota factory		this mark also occurs with the letter S
	1530		c. 1520
	c. 1530		c. 1525
	c. 1525		
	c. 1520		
	1527		c. 1540

MARK.	DESCRIPTION.	MARK.	DESCRIPTION.
·M·F·F	**Faenza**	·B· ·M·	**Faenza** Baldasara Manara. 1534
	c. 1530	*Baldāsara manara faentine*	
·F·	c. 1525 (? Casa Pirota)		
·P·	1533		
AF·IƷ	Mark of Vergiliotto 17th cent.		1527
ṼR·Æ·			
	1550		
ÆR	with the word FAENZA		Perhaps the mark of the Atanasio factory in Faenza
	? Faenza c. 1525	I R	1508
		F·R	1520-30
		Enniusraynerius F.F.	Ennius Raynerius Faentinus faciebat 1575
S M 1506			
B·M·F	Baldasara Manara Faventinus (or *fecit*) c. 1530	M	also inscribed Giovano Brama di Parlerma 1546 in faenza

MARK.	DESCRIPTION.	MARK.	DESCRIPTION.
	Faenza		**Forli**
fato in faienze in Botega di M° fran.	1556	*Ī la botega da M° Iero da Forli*	
Io Ant Romanino Cimatti de Favesc	1556 Cimatti or Cimani		(? Early Diruta)
Zacharia Valaressi 1651 in Faenza			
F B F	Francesco Ballanti 18th cent.	AF·I(*n*)FOR(*l*)I	
R B F	Benini fabrique 1777-8	RAVENA	**Ravenna**
	Forli	*Thomas Masselli Ferrarien fec*	**Ferrara**
		in Rimino 1535	**Rimini**
			1535
	1485-90	*Iulio da Urbino in botega de mastro alisandro in arimino*	1535
	1523	*In Venetia in Cōtrada di Sta Polo in botega di M° Ludovico*	**Venice**

MARK.	DESCRIPTION.	MARK.	DESCRIPTION.
	Venice		**Venice**
✝ ✝	? Mark of Mᵒ Ludovico c. 1540		Marks of the Bertolini factory c. 1753
Io Stefano Barcella Veneziano Pinx			
Mᵒ Jacomo da Pesaro	In Stᵒ Barnaba in Venice 1542		
Guido Merlingo Vasaro da Urbino	In San Polo in Venice 1542		
AoLASDINR	1543		
Mᵒ Francesco da Castel Durante	In Sᵃ Thoma in Venice 1545	S G I B	c. 1750
dt 1545	,,	B S 1760	Probably Venetian Marks 18th cent.
in venezia in chastello	1546		
G	1571-1622		
Zener domenigo da Venecia	1568		
Baldantonio in Venecia	1551		
Bariselio	1587	F.S.N	
Jacomo Vasellaro	1593	VC	
R. da Madre Suor Zuana	1596		
D. M. SEIMO			
G.L.P. 1667			

MARK.	DESCRIPTION.	MARK.	DESCRIPTION.
Giovani Batista da faenza in Verona M	**Verona** 1563	1737 *Fabbrica de Torino*	**Turin**
	Milan		Rosetti factory
	Pasquale Rubati 1762 ——		1629
	Felice Clerici 1745 ——		Uncertain Turin marks
		T.	
		T.G.	
		Borgano	c. 1823
		Eredi Imoda	
G.A.O.F 1708 M A M	**Pavia**	*Luigi Richard e C.*	
		GRATA PAGLIA FE : TAVR :	
	c. 1710		**Vinovo** Mark of Vittorio Amadeo Gioanetti c. 1776
	Turin Arms of Savoy under a crown	M. M.	**Mondovi** Benedetto Musso 19th cent.
		B G	Giuseppe Besio
Fatta in Torino	1577	M A	Annibale Musso

MARK.	DESCRIPTION.	MARK.	DESCRIPTION.
D.O.N. P.A.R.I.S.T.O.E.D. A.T.R.A.V.I.S.I.O. S. M. 1595	**Treviso** 1538 **Bassano** ? Simone Marioni	**GB** NOVE	**Nove** G. Baroni Early 19th cent.
1G^ F^F. 1569 P. BAS+ANO		S.I.G	1750
Antonio TeriEi in	Antonio Terchi	N·OUE Gio^ni Marconi pinx. ⸸ 𝓈	A star of six points alone is a Nove mark
Bassano		NICO LETI	**Padua**
B° Terctj	Bartolomeo Terchi (See p. 11)	N·+·F.	1563
Bassano		1564 + a padoa	
	mark used by Terchi	+ X	c. 1555
J	mark used by Manardi, late 17th cent.	*Candiana* 1620	**Candiana** On imitations of Turkish faïence
NB	Manardi at Bassano	S.E.C.	**Lodi**
Angaron 1779	incised	M Lodi 1764	
No:ue G·B·A·B:	**Nove** Giovanni Battista Antonibon	*Fabbrica di Rosetti in Lodi*	,,
GAB	Early 18th cent.	*Felix Crevani fecit* 1767	

MARK.	DESCRIPTION.	MARK.	DESCRIPTION.
	Savona		**Savona**
	Mark of Siccardi c. 1700		S. Rubatto
	also a star of five points		
	18th cent.		Mark of Chiodo c. 1667
	? Girolamo Salomini		Mark of Bartolomeo Guidobono
	Luigi Levantino c. 1670		,,
			Mark of G. Salomone
	Mark of Levantino		Mark of Pescetto, also three fishes.
			Falcon, mark of Folco
	also on piece dated 1751		1729
	with signature of A. Ratti		Siccardi (see above)

MARK.	DESCRIPTION.	MARK.	DESCRIPTION.
	Savona		**Castelli**
M. Borelli A. S. 1735	Borelli factory		= Bernardino Gentile fece
Jacques Borelli	1779		
		Bernardino Gentile	1670
	Albissola	C. G. P.	Carmine Gentile pinxit
		Gentile p.	
	Naples	G. Rocco di Castelli	1732
	Marks of F. Brandi 1654	Capelleti	
		Fuina	
Carlo Coccorese	1784	Luc. Antº Ciañico	
		Math. Rossetti	
F D V N	Del Vecchio Naples. 19th cent.		Naples 1760 to present day
M · C ·			
	Castelli		,,
C. A. G. pi.	Carl Antonio Grue 17th cent.		
D. Francisci Antonii Xarerii Grue	1735		Mark of Cantagalli of Florence
L. G. P.	Liborio Grue († 1776)		
Grve p	Saverio Grue († 1799)		Modern
1757	One of the Grue family		

MARK.	DESCRIPTION.	MARK.	DESCRIPTION.
A	Uncertain marks ? Diruta or Viterbo 1600-20	 F	Marks on porcelain made at Florence under the patronage of Grand Duke Francesco Maria, who died 1587 The first represents the cupola of the Cathedral of Florence :
·L̊ª	? Urbino		
1540 TÆ			
1547 ·ESIONE T·Z		Ⓜ Ⓜ Ⓕ Ⓔ Ⓓ Ⓘ	the second the arms of the Medici
1551 ·S· ᵛA⸲			
GEO·BAŤA·MERCATI 1649	Name of an artist of Citta S. Sepolcro, whose design was copied on a plate		
ᏕᴍB Gᴹ	? Monograms of the same		
·C · F	? Castelli		On a plate which has also the first mark All are painted in blue under the glaze
Fabrica di Bonpencier			

MARK.	DESCRIPTION.	MARK.	DESCRIPTION.
Ven^a	**Venice** Marks of the Vezzi factory 1719-40 h.p. and s.p. p. in blue	⚓ *I. G^a* ⚓	**Venice** Cozzi factory p. in red
VEN:		*A E W* *I W* *A^G^*	also with initials G. M.
	p. in blue		
		Fortunato Tolerazzi Fece Venesia 1763	at the Hewelcke factory (1758-63) inc.
Ludovico Ortolani Veneto dipinse nella Fabrica di Porcelana in Venetia	p. in lake	V W ⚭	**Vische** 1765-68
Ven^a A. G. 1726	p. in red		
C^P a L i:10		✡	**Doccia** Factory founded by the Marchese Carlo Ginori in 1735 and continued to the present day
		P.F	In a circle initials of Fanciullacci
Venezia Fab^a Geminiano Cozzi	The Cozzi factory 1764-1812 p. in red s.p.	GINORI	s.p. at first h.p. afterwards also pottery

MARK.	DESCRIPTION.	MARK.	DESCRIPTION.
	Le Nove 1762-1825		**Capo di Monte** (Naples) The factory was removed to Naples about 1771. These marks are after that date. s.p. till c. 1780. Marks p. in blue and inc. The company carried on till 1834
✳	p. in red and blue s.p.		
✴			
𝓕	*Cf.* marks on Le Nove pottery on p. 19 p. in gold		Cypher of King Ferdinand p. in red
✳		*Giordano*	Incised on figures : names of modellers
F.F.	**Treviso** s.p. Fratelli Fontebasso p. in gold	*Apiello*	
Treviſo 1799			and other forms of the fleur-de-lys : supposed to be early Capo di Monte marks, but probably Buen Retiro (see p. 91) p. in blue
⚓ (cross-anchor) 1776	**Vinovo** 1776-1815 "hybrid porcelain" p. in grey	*BG*	Giustiniani factory (see p. 21)
✝	p. in black		
✝ MIA	p. in grey and inc.		
✝			? Vicenza
D G	Dr. Gioanetti (see p. 18)	W	
Caraſsus pinx	p. in gold	ESTE +1783+	**Este** s.p.

Mark.	Description.	Mark.	Description.
	Italian maiolica		**German faïence**
fabbrica Magrin *Pesaro*	Magrini & Co. 1870 ——	ℂ𝐿	Georg Leubold (Hamburg) 1622
		WR	**Nuremberg** a painter's initials c. 1680
F S . C	Fabbrica di Santa Cristina Milan c. 1780	B ℐ.S	18th cent.
			Early 18th cent.
Dᵣ Fräc Antˢ Grue f. Neap. 1710	**Naples** F. A. Grue (See p. 21)		,,
del Vecchio N	19th cent.	J: A: Marx 1735	John Andreas at the Marx factory p. 29
	? Giustiniani	Künc :berg ·L·	**Künersberg** p. 24c c. 1745
		Franz	,,
		SCHRAMBERG	**Schramberg** 1820 ——
	on modern maiolica	*Belvedere Manufactur in Warschau*	**Warsaw** c. 1790
I.G.P.F 1627 G.G.P.F 1638	on porcelain probably made at Pisa p. in blue	BK *Larner*	**Bayreuth** p. 30
✝ ⧧		B.F.S C	Fränkel & Schreck 1745 ——
		ψ	? Von Loewenfeldt
		ℱ 1682	Mark of Faber, decorator

Mark.	Description.	Mark.	Description.
⊕ **I H**	**Höchst** faïence (p. 30)	$\cancel{E}$	? Lambrecht de Costere. Antwerp 1583
CN	Höchst painter's initials		
D	**Hamburg** Early 18th cent.	P P	**Proskau** (Silesia) 1763 ——
Rendsbürg	**Rendsburg** 1765-1818	$\mathcal{D}\,P.$	
Duve		$\dfrac{P}{6}$	D. P. 1770-83
SLfwig $\mathcal{CE}$	**Schleswig** 1754-1814	$P+$	
Anno 1786 ys 21 Marts olsesdof	**Oldesloe**	C.K. 17 P. 47	**Salzburg**
M²⁰ GUISHARD SHUICHARD	**Magdeburg** Early 19th cent.	Jan Derks	**Delft** 17th cent.
Fotg.dam 1.7.40	**Prussia**	$\mathcal{G}$	G. L. Kruyk 1645
K	Königsberg c. 1775-1811	*D. Tenniers invent. I. Aalmis pinx. a Rotterdam 1777*	**Rotterdam** on tiles
HE	Hofrat Errenreich	*Doctor Grauers faÿance fabrique*	**Kellinghusen** c. 1800
C.F. de Wolfsbeurg pinxit.1729	porcelain decorator	$\dfrac{V}{CB7Q}$ 6f	**Copenhagen** 1727-c. 1770

Mark.	Description.	Mark.	Description.
O𝕱	**Offenbach** 1739 onwards	VR	**Wrisbergholzen** 18th and early 19th cent.
K HD	**Kelsterbach** (see p. 38) c. 1760-1830	Z M	**Zerbst** 1728——
wb JW.	**Wiesbaden** 1770-1795	A Sverin A·S K	**Schwerin** c. 1750——
K·B· ℬ	**Künersberg** c. 1745	Jever ιι	**Jever** 18th cent.
	Göppingen c. 1741-1800	V.H.	**Brunswick** Von Hartelmann and Von Horn 1711-49
I $\frac{I}{3}$	**Ludwigsburg** see p. 37 c. 1750-1824	B⅋R R&C I	Behling and Reichard, 1749-50 Rabe & Co. 1773-1776 Chely's, c. 1750
ℒ	**Baden-Baden** c. 1750-1778	ζ· A	**Eckernförde** at Criseby 1758-64
·P·San	**Potsdam** see p. 32	$\frac{F}{H}$ $\frac{F}{H}$	**Frankfort** (on Oder) c. 1763-90
M	**Münden** (p. 32) or Magdeburg		

Mark.	Description.	Mark.	Description.
	Reval 1780 92		**Copenhagen** Wolff 1722-27
			Kastrup c. 1754-1800
	Dresden c. 1710-84	G·B·S.	**Delft** New Saracen's Head
	Erfurt c. 1717-93		**Three Bells** J. von der Laan
	Dorotheenthal c. 1710-1805		**Meissen** porcelain Friedrich Augustus c. 1733
	Abtsbessingen 18th cent.		**Fürstenberg** p. 36
C.B	**Coburg** 18th cent.	N.S.	**Ottweiler** Nassau- Saarbrücken c. 1770
	Gera c. 1750		**Bayreuth** (p. 35) J. F. Metzsch
	Cassel 1680-1788		**Vienna** (p. 40) c. 1735
	Fulda c. 1750	*Iacobus Helchis fecit*	
			decorators marks

GERMAN POTTERY

A NUMBER of potters in Germany and Switzerland from the sixteenth century onwards were engaged in the manufacture of elaborate stove-tiles, usually ornamented with reliefs in sunk panels and coloured with slips, glazes, and tin enamel ; brown, yellow, green, blue, maganese purple, and white were the principal colours used. The manufacture of tin-glazed faïence after the Italian and Dutch styles was common in most parts of Germany in the seventeenth and eighteenth centuries ; and a certain amount of slip-decorated and graffiato earthenware was made in South Germany, at Gennep in Luxembourg, and at Schaffhausen in Switzerland, in the eighteenth century.

In the Rhenish provinces a large stoneware industry developed in the sixteenth century at Siegburg, Raeren, Cologne, Frechen, and elsewhere, and during the two following centuries at Grenzhausen in Nassau. The typical Rhenish stoneware varies from white to freckled brown, and is ornamented with panels in low relief made in moulds and applied, as well as with stamped and incised decoration : the ware was glazed with salt, and sometimes coloured with patches of cobalt blue and maganese purple. The cutting of moulds for the reliefs was an important branch of this industry, and most of the marks are those of the mould-cutters, and appear in relief in the panels. Bottles with a bearded mark on the neck, known as Bellarmines or Greybeards, are the commonest specimens of Rhenish stoneware. The tall, tapering tankards of white Siegburg ware are among the best examples of this class. Another variety, made chiefly at Kreussen, is heavily painted in enamel colours.

GERMAN PORCELAIN

THE secret of true or hard-paste porcelain, after the manner of the Chinese, was discovered about 1707 at Dresden by J. F. Böttger, an alchemist, in the employ of Augustus II. of Poland, Elector of Saxony. He discovered about the same time the method of making a fine red stoneware, now known as Böttger ware, but called by him red porcelain. This ware was finished by polishing on the lathe, or covering with a black glaze and enriching with gold and silver ornament or engraving. Böttger and his secrets were transferred in 1710 to Meissen, where he started the celebrated Meissen porcelain factory under strict surveillance. The process, however, could not be kept hidden, and escaped workmen carried the secret first to Vienna and afterwards to all parts of Germany. Factories sprung up in one principality after another under the protection of the ruling houses, who vied with each other during the eighteenth century in the production of true porcelain. All the German porcelain is hard paste, varying in fineness according to the sources of the porcelain clay. The finest material was obtained from Aue in Saxony, and a coarser earth mined near Passau produced the greyer and inferior wares made in the Thuringian factories at the end of the eighteenth century. Each factory had its distinctive mark usually painted in blue under the glaze, though among the minor factories, particularly those of the Thuringian district, there was a tendency to use marks suspiciously similar to the Meissen crossed swords. The latter mark is sometimes found with one or two cuts across it: this signifies that the ware was faulty and rejected by the Meissen factory as unfit for decoration, and any ornament on pieces so marked must have been added elsewhere.

Mark.	Description.	Mark.	Description.
R.A. 1589	Marks on stove tiles	L	1589
ADAM VOGT 1626	Augsburg	P V 1605	Peter Vlack
HANS KRAUT	Villingen 1578	**Raeren**	
HK	,,	B M 1577	Baldem Menneken
CW 1582		I M 1578	Jan Menneken
ICD		E M 1596	Edmonds Menneken
	1550	I F	Jan Fasz
	Siegburg	I E 1576	Jan Emens
	Marks of the potters and mould carvers	shield with I E M	The same with "merchant's mark"
A K	Anno Knütgen		
B K 1557	Bertram Knütgen		
F T		E E 1586	
C K	Christian Knütgen (1563-1605)	G E 1590	George Emens
P K 1570	Peter Knütgen	P E	Peter Emens c. 1585
M P D 1551		W E	c. 1609
L W 1573	? Lorenz Wolter	L K I K	Kran or Kalb family
I M	1573	W K H K	
C F I V S		E K	Engel Kran 1584
shield 1588 / 4 A B	Monograms of this kind are known as "merchant's marks"	D P 1571 R	D. Pitz Raeren
		H H 1595	Hans Hilgers
		T W	Tilman Wolf 17th cent.
		T W K	
		I T 1601	

MARK.	DESCRIPTION.	MARK.	DESCRIPTION.
	Raeren		**Höhr-Grenzhausen**
W Z		G R	Gills Remy
C P		P R	Peter Remy
L W		W R	Wilhelm Remy
H B E B	Baldens family 17th cent.	L B	Leonhardt Blum 1632
I A	Jean Allers	A K	Anno Knütgen 1590
M H	Melsior Honckebour		
[monogram W E]	? Willem Emens	[circular monogram M & M Gr]	Grenzhausen modern
[monogram]	? Willens		**Westerwald**
		I C	c. 1620
		I K	Jan Kalb 1618
		I	
H S	Hubert Schiffer (modern)	M P	**Bouffioux** ? Pierre Morfroy
	Höhr-Grenzhausen in Nassau	J R	Jean Rifflet
M 1597	Menneken	J B	Jean Bertrand
I M	Jan Menneken	J A	Jean Allers
L M	Lambertus Menneken	[monogram]	**Cologne** 17th cent.
I E M	Jan Edmonds Menneken		
Johannes Mennechen Höhr 1790			
K B L Höhr	18th cent.	[anchor] [NF monogram]	Late 18th cent.

MARK.	DESCRIPTION.	MARK.	DESCRIPTION.
CASPAR VEST	**Kreussen** Stoneware	𝕸𝕶	**Nuremberg** ? Kordenbusch
𝒜		*G. Kordenbusch*	
HANS CHRISTOPH VEST	1600	J. G. K.	
GEORGIUS VEST	1603	B. K. K.	
ADAM SCHARF	1644	G. K.	
M J W C			
I V	Vogel 1628	NB K: NB F NB 4.	
C L M E L		G. F. GREBNER	1720
M M C		*Gluer* 1723	
		Johann Sebalt Franz	
MATTHÆUS SCHRÖNVOGEL ZU BASSAU	On ware made at **Passau** 1638, in the Kreussen style	*Stebner*	1771
		IOH : SCHAPER	1665 a decorator on Hanau porcelain
A C A M	On Saxon wares	I 𝓢	J. Schaper
	Nuremberg 1712-1840	*M. Schmid* 1722	a follower of Schaper
HERR CHRISTOPH MARX	1712	J L F	1688
JOHANN CONRADT ROMEDI	,,	𝓐⊣𝚰	Abraham Helmhack 1680-1724
Ströbel: **B**	In the Marx factory 1730	B ≡ W ↑ 𝓢	**Schretzheim** near Ellwangen early 18th cent.
N. Possinger	1725		

MARK.	DESCRIPTION.	MARK.	DESCRIPTION.
	Schretzheim	ANTONIO CARDINAL GERRIT LONNE PETER MENTEN	**Gennep** (in Luxembourg) 18 cent. Graffiato ware and slip ware
Matthias Rosa in *Anspath*	**Ansbach** c. 1710-1810	*J. S* *j. HA*	names and initials of potters
		Pieter Heichens fecit *in Berlot* 1777	
Pinxit F. G. Fliegel *Arnstadt* 1775	Dorotheenthal by Arnstadt		**Höchst** c. 1745-1798
göggingen *H S*	**Göggingen** near Augsburg 1748——, style of Savona		
Baijreuthe *K Flu·*	**Bayreuth** c. 1720-1835		Marks of Zeschinger, who sometimes signs his full name
B K·	Knöller (1720-40)		
$\frac{BK}{c}$			
BP *·BP*	Pfeiffer 1747-1767		**Dirmstein** late 18th cent.
B P·F	? Pfeiffer and Fränkel, c. 1747		**Damm** near Aschaffen- berg, c. 1825
ANTONIUS BERNARDUS VON VEHLEN	**Gennep** 1770	*D*	**Flörsheim** c. 1765 onwards C. Machenhauer 1781
PM WM	? Gennep 1715	C M	

MARK.	DESCRIPTION.	MARK.	DESCRIPTION.
JH *HK*	**Frankenthal** Hannong 18th cent.	*İ İ*	**Hamburg** c. 1628-1680 and 18th cent.
H *H 872*		*Johann Otto Lessel sculpsit et Pinxit Hamburg* 1756	
$\frac{M}{7}$ *t*	**Mainz** 18th cent.	*Kiel Buchwald Director Abr: Leihamer fecit*	**Kiel** 1758-c. 1792
B W.			
W. R *1731*	**Marburg**	*1778 B: Direct: A: fec:*	
⚓	**Poppelsdorf** 18th cent.	$\frac{K}{B.Dit.}$ *A L 69*	
👑 *M 1755*	**Bonn**	$\frac{K}{B}{L}$ $\frac{K}{J}{k}$	
H *HB*	**Hanau** (1661-1805) H. Bally (1680-90)	$\frac{c}{k}{AL}$ 681 $\frac{K}{B}{R.C.}$	
VA	Van Alphen	$\frac{S}{CB}$ $\frac{S}{H}$	**Schleswig** 1754-1814
⊂	factory mark	$\frac{S}{R}$ $\frac{S}{R}{B}$	**Rambusch** 1753-1801
HV. XX	1740-86		

MARK.	DESCRIPTION.	MARK.	DESCRIPTION.
	Eckernförde 1764-c. 1785 OEB = Otte, Eckernförde, Buchwald A. Leihammer		**Lesum** Vielstich (1755-94)
	Stockelsdorff Buchwald 1773		
			Mosbach 1770-1803
			Münden in Hannover 18th cent.
	? Hadensee or Stralsund		**Kellinghusen** c. 1765-1850
			1796
	Stralsund N.E. Prussia 1768		**Fulda** (1740-58)
			Rheinsberg Lüdecker, Rheinsberg. 1762 onwards
	"		**Potsdam** c. 1680-1810
	(this mark also assigned to Marieberg, Sweden)		**Frankfort** (on Main) 1661-c. 1780

MARK.	DESCRIPTION.	MARK.	DESCRIPTION.
	Meissen Marks incised on Böttger's wares 1707-1719		**Meissen** "Caduceus" mark, properly the rod of Æsculapius. p. in blue and purple 1727-35
			Cypher of Augustus II. of Poland, Elector of Saxony. p. in blue and purple 1725-40
	Imitation Chinese and Japanese marks on Meissen porcelain early 18th cent. p. in blue	 *N=Z85* w	An early mark in gold
		George Ernst Keil. *Meissen Inv. 6 Jŭli* 1724	In an ornamental escutcheon
			The cross swords from the Arms of Saxony used from 1725 onwards. p. in blue, rarely in gold, purple or red
  Z 90. w.	(Incised mark on porcelain in the royal collection at Dresden)		Inc.

MARK.	DESCRIPTION.	MARK.	DESCRIPTION.
	Meissen		**Meissen**
	K. H. C. W. = Königliche Hof Conditorei, Warsaw (Royal Court Confectionery). p. in purple		
			The dot used mostly from 1756-74
	Königliche Porzellan Manufactur. p. in purple 1723-30 also K. P. F.		The star used during the directorship of Count Camillo Marcolini and a few years after 1774-1816
		J. J. Kaendler	Sculptor and modeller 1731-74
	private decorators' initials.		Workmen's signs impressed or painted, painters' and gilders' marks
	Impressed : very rare		
			A pheasant, in gold
			Loehnig pinxit. p. in purple
C. F. Herold invt : et fecit a meissē 1750		*Lauche fecit Dresden*	painter's name

Mark.	Description.	Mark.	Description.
	Meissen		**Ansbach**
K	Kretzschmar or Kohnberger		
E	Eggebrecht		p. in blue
L	Lindner		
Mö	Möbius		
B	Berger		
H	Hammer or Hempel		
iAW *Auffenwürg*	Marks of private decorators J. A. Auffenwerth.		Arms of Ansbach
Busch 1749	Busch, canon of Hildesheim, who etched his designs with a diamond point	*Metzsch* 1748 *Bayr.*	**Bayreuth** p. in grey
W *AB 1726*	I. A. Bottengruber of Breslau (Wrattislau)	*Bayreuth, Fec. Jucht*	Jucht, a painter. p. in blue
			Höchst 1746-96 p. in blue or colours, or impressed
	Ansbach c. 1760 The eagle of Brandenburg, to which family the Margraves of Ansbach belonged		Marks of Zeschinger (see also p. 30)
A *A* *A*		*R*	p. in blue

Mark.	Description.	Mark.	Description.
	Höchst Joseph Schneider imp.		**Frankenthal** Cypher of Carl Theodor, Elector Palatine. p. in blue (1762-99)
	Mark of a figure repairer (*not* Melchior)		? Frankenthal. p. in lilac
	Damm (see p. 30) where the Höchst moulds were used from about 1840		,, Von Recum c. 1800
	Fürstenberg 1750-c. 1850 p. in blue		Mark used at **Pfalz-Zweibrücken** 1769-75 (and at **Gutenbrunn** 1767-69)
	Horse of Brunswick imp. **Frankenthal** 1755-c. 1800 Lion of the Palatinate and monogram of J. A. Hannong. p. in blue		**Nymphenburg** 1761 to present day (at Neudeck 1753) Arms of Bavaria imp. I. A. H. = Johann Adam Huber
	Paul Hannong		p. in blue (1753-61)
			1799-1810 imp.
	p. in blue		= Churfürstliche Hof Zehrgaden (Electoral Court Store-room). Plain brown

Mark.	Description.	Mark.	Description.
C. H. Conditorëÿ 17 1771	**Nymphenburg** = Churfürstliche Hof Conditorei (Electoral Court Confectionery). p. in brown	W W	**Berlin** (1750 to present day) Initial of Wegeli (1750-57)
C. H. Silberkamer	,, plate-chamber	Ç.	Gotzkowski (1761-63). p. in blue
	p. in grey	I I ⊹	Sceptre of Elector of Brandenburg 1763-1837: with dots Jan. 1837. p. in blue
	imp. c. 1780	KPM	P. with sceptre and eagle from 1832 Königliche Porzellan Manufactur
Amberg. 1774	Private decorator. p. in lilac	KPM.	1834-1844
	Ludwigsburg 1758-1824 Arms of Würtemberg, 3 stags' horns. p. in blue	KPM	In red and brown (1823-32) in blue (1844-1847)
L	L.		1847-49. And with sceptre (1849-80) The eagle also used by Schuman of **Moabit** with his name from 1832
	Stag's horn from the arms of Würtemberg.		From 1870
CC	Cypher of Charles, Duke of Würtemberg (1737-93). p. in blue		From 1882. Seger Porzellan
CC	F R, cypher of Frederick I. King of Würtemberg (1805-16). p. in red.	Sgr.P	Painter's mark in blue 1803-10, in red 1821-23

MARK.	DESCRIPTION.	MARK.	DESCRIPTION.
	Kelsterbach c. 1760-72 H D = Hess Darmstadt. p. in blue		**Closter Veilsdorf** 1765-c. 1825 Arms of Saxony. p. in blue
	Limbach (Thuringia) 1762 onwards. Crossed Ls used Grossbreitenbach till 1788. p. in blue		c. 1787
	Limbach		c. 1783 Also the cross swords of Meissen
	Trefoil (seal of G. Greiner) used at Limbach and Grossbreitenbach from 1788 onwards and at Ilmenau		**Gotha** (1767 onwards) 1767-1795. p. in blue 1795-1805. Mark of Rotteberg the director
	Factory of **Grossbreiten- bach** dates from 1779 to present day. inc.		1805-1830 St. in red (? rebus for Henneberg) 1830-60
	Wallendorf c. 1778 p. in blue		? Gotha or Gera
	,,		**Ilmenau** 1777-1788. p. in blue
	,,		1787
	Volkstedt 1762-87 used hayfork (from arms of Rudolstadt and cross swords		c. 1800 1788-92
	Mark of Nonne at Volkstedt 1787 onwards. p. in blue		Nonne and Roesch c. 1800

Mark.	Description.	Mark.	Description.
	Rauenstein 1783-1860. p. in black		gilder's mark on ? Ansbach porcelain
	c. 1787. p. in blue		**Schlaggenwald** (Bohemia) 1792 onwards
	Modern mark		Lippe and Hesse. p. or stamped
	Gera c. 1780 *Cf.* Gotha		**Thun-Klösterle** 1793 onwards p. in blue
	? Sitzerode		
	Fulda 1768-c. 1790 Fürstlich Fuldaisch. p. in blue		
	Cross from arms of prince-bishop of Fulda		**Prague** imp. 1793 onwards **Teinitz** Wrtby 1793 onwards imp. (Pottery)
	p. in black ? Fulda		**Giesshübel** (by Karlsbad) 1793 onwards. BK imp. since 1815
	Potschappel (near Dresden) T for Thieme. 19th cent.		**Dalwitz** 1804 onwards imp.
	Uncertain marks		
			Kodau (Karlsbad) 1810 onwards imp.

Mark.	Description.	Mark.	Description.
(mark)	**Altrohlau** (Karlsbad) from 1813 onwards imp.	*(shield mark)*	**Vienna** (1718 onwards) Austrian shield used from 1749 in blue; impressed from 1744-49 and after 1827. Since 1784 last two numerals of the date are often impressed as well; and three numerals in the 19th cent.
AN	A. Nowotny	*Vienne 12 July 1721*	
(mark)	**Elbogen** 1815 onwards. p. in blue till 1833, and then imp. Haidinger brothers	*Ant:^{us} Anreiter* $\overset{\circ}{V}Z: 1755$	Antonius, Anreiter, painter
B:	**Budau** 1825 onwards mostly p. in blue	*Bottengruber Siles:f Viennæ 1730* *Wratis: A^{o} 17z8* *Bottengruberf*	I. A. Bottengruber who also painted in his own establishment in Breslau. (See p. 35)
AL			
S	**Schelten** 1820 onwards P for Palme imp.	**HEREND** *(shield mark)*	**Herend** in Hungary 19th cent. Celebrated for copies of Oriental, Sèvres, Capo di Monte, and other porcelains. Imp.
XI C F 4	**Pirkenhammer** Carl Fischer c. 1840 imp.		
F&B	Fischer and Reichenbeck	*Hollitsch* *2* *D: P.Ht.ce*	**Hollitsch** faïence and earthenware 1743-1827
F&R			
KLUM	**Klum** imp.	**H** $\underset{M:20}{1769}$ **HH** **'HK'**	
Neumark	**Neumark**	*Ko* *4*	
Klentsch	**Klentsch**	*Hf* *HP*	and other initials combined with **H**
W HARDMUTH	**Budweis** The last four from about 1820 imp.		

Mark.	Description.	Mark.	Description.
+S SB J M P J P P J	**Salzburg** 1736-1815 faïence Moser 1736-77 J. Pisotti 1777-1814		**Fünfkirchen** (Pécs) W. Zsolnay 1855 onwards (lustred wares)
REINTHAL I. R. E F 1812	**Gmunden** 1740-1820 J. Reinthal E. Fötinger		**The Hague** Modern porcelain works in the suburb of *Rosenburg den Haag*
M. K. 1634	**Auspitz**		**Mettlach** Villeroy and Boch. Mark on modern pottery (See p. 51)
	Frain late 18th cent		
	Znaim Klammerth 19th cent.	 H & Cº L FRANCE 	**Limoges** Marks of Haviland and Co., an American firm of porcelain manufacturers Mark on modern Italian majolica

MARK.	DESCRIPTION.	MARK.	DESCRIPTION.
Luplau fec 1781	**Copenhagen** porcelain Anton Carl Luplau modeller.	*Eneret*	= patent : on Danish porcelain
Ondrup	Ondrup, painter 1779-87	M 530 C *Thun*	Thun or Thoune, Switzerland 19th cent.
A. Hald *A. H.*	Andreas Hald modeller (1781-97)	J. Æ.	**France** Jarry at Aprey p. 67
HOLM 1780	J. J. Holm sculptor	HB *Quimper*	Quimper p. 67
J: C. Bayer	Johan Christoph Bayer, painter 1768-1812	CHOISY	Choisy-le-roi early 19th cent. creamware
	Jacob Schmidt modeller 1779-1807	P & H	Paillart and Hautin 1824-36
	Hans Meehl modeller c. 1791		Chantilly h. p. porcelain
HM	Jensen, painter c. 1820	P.	? Potter late 18th cent.
≡ J	Lyngbe, painter c. 1830	*Teuillet*	Paris, 19th cent. p. 76
≡ L	Arnold Krog, art-director 1885 onwards		**Spain**
	C. F. Liisberg, painter, etc., 1885-1909		? Malaga 15th cent.
	V. Engelhardt chemist 1892 onwards		
(crown over waves)	on modern copies of early wares.	(triangle in circle with I)	Buen Retiro p. 92

THE NETHERLANDS, SCANDINAVIA, RUSSIA, SWITZERLAND, AND ALSACE-LORRAINE

THE tin-glazed earthenware made at Delft in Holland is so celebrated that the word delft has come to be used as a generic term for the stanniferous wares of the North of Europe. Though the use of tin glaze was understood in the Netherlands at least a century earlier, it was about the year 1600 that the manufacture developed in Delft. The processes used at Delft were in most respects similar to those of the Italian maiolica potters (see p. 1), but the results were very different owing to the divergent styles of decoration affected in the two countries. The object of the potters of Delft was to make a ware resembling blue and white Oriental porcelain. Hence the predominance of Oriental forms and of blue painting after the style of the Chinese. Towards the end of the seventeenth century coloured ornament in "Old Japan" style came into fashion, and still later enamel painting on the glaze was adopted. The marks of the earlier wares are usually in blue : the coloured specimens were often marked in colours or gold. The marks are as far as possible grouped in factories each of which had its sign, like an inn, *e.g.* The Three Bells, The Flower Pot, The Claw, etc. The remaining marks are arranged chronologically, the last being that of Jan Van Putten & Co., with whom the old Delft industry may be said to have ended in the first half of the nineteenth century, though imitations of the old wares are made at this day. The manufacture of tin-glazed wares showing the influence of Delft spread rapidly over the North of Europe ; England, Scandinavia, and the North of Germany numbered many factories, while in France the manufacture became national and developed a character of its own. The tin-enamelled wares died out gradually owing to the improvements in the making of porcelain and the cheaper and more serviceable

43

English earthenwares invented in Staffordshire at the end of the eighteenth century.

A red unglazed ware after the manner of the Chinese " buccaro " was made in Holland by de Milde and de Calve late in the seventeenth century.

A few hard-paste porcelain factories were established in Holland and Belgium towards the end of the eighteenth century, and an important manufacture of soft-paste porcelain, after the French fashion, flourished at Tournay from 1750-1799.

The principal Scandinavian potteries were at Herreböe, Rörstrand (a district of Stockholm), and at Marieberg. Tin-enamelled faïence after the fashion of Delft was the chief product, though porcelain also was made at Marieberg for some years.[1] The hard-paste porcelain of Copenhagen was first made in 1772, and the factory holds an important position for its artistic wares at the present time. It had been preceded by the manufacture of soft paste, examples of which are very rare.

Russian porcelain was made principally at the Royal factory in St. Petersburg, and by Gardner and Popoff in Moscow : hard paste, after the manner of Meissen, was made at both places.

Stove-tiles, slip-wares, and tin-enamelled faïence were produced in considerable quantity in Switzerland in the seventeenth and eighteenth centuries, chiefly at Winterthur, Zurich, Schaffhausen ; and porcelain works flourished at Zurich and Nyon, making chiefly hard-paste porcelain, though soft paste was tried for a time at Zurich.

In Alsace-Lorraine the principal factories were those of Strassburg, Hagenau, and Niderviller where good faïence and hard-paste porcelain were made in the eighteenth century. The Strassburg faïence is noted for its rococo forms and its enamelled decoration resembling the painting on porcelain. Fine earthenware and terra-cottas were made at Lunéville and at Niderviller, the figures and groups modelled by Cyfflé at the former place, and Lemire at the latter being justly celebrated.

[1] The factory at Rorstrand has for many years produced many varieties of porcelain, earthenware, and stove-tiles. Its present-day porcelain is worthy of note.

Mark.	Description.	Mark.	Description.
$E	**The Alpha** Samuel van Eenhorn	G·d K	Gillis de Koning 1721
JvDH ~	J. van der Heul, 1701	HDK DSK	Hendrick de Koning Thomas Spaandonck, 1764
Æ/ITD DEX	Jan Theunis Dextra, 1759	PVS	**The Flowerpot** Pieter van der Stroom, 1693
Æ/I:H	Jacobus Halder Andriaensz	l'lompot RB	= Blompot Paulus van der Burgh (or Verburg) 1759
D. K boot	**The Boat** Dirck van der Kest, 1675	J R J in 't Fortuyn	**The Fortune** Joris Oosterwijck 1706
IDA	Johann den Appel 1759	P VI. B· W vDB	Pieter van den Briel, 1759 Widow van den Briel
(image)	**The Claw**	MB	**The Four Roman Heroes** Mathijs Boender 1713
C.V:S	Cornelia van Schoonhoven or Cornelius van Schagen, 1694	T H ART t'hart	**The Stag**
B·V·S LVS	Bettje and Lysbet van Schoonhoven 1702	HVMD	Hendrick van Middeldijk, 1764
K VD	Kornelis van Dyck, 1759	MDK	,,
XK	**The Double Flagon** Amerensie van Kessel, 1675	P	**The Metal Pot** Pieter van Kessel 1634 Lambertus Cleffius, 1667
VE	Louwys Fictoor 1689	Æ VE VE	Lambertus van Eenhorn, 1691

Mark.	Description.	Mark.	Description.
C VK	**The Metal Pot** Cornelis van der Kloot, 1695	JIO H	**The Porcelain Bottle** Jan Sicktis van den Houk, 1659
MP	Pieter Paree 1759	PD	Pieter van Doorne, 1759
IVH	**The New Saracen's Head** Johannes Verhagen, 1759	HL	Johannes Harlees 1770
	The Old Saracen's Head c. 1700		
iK	Jacobus Kool 1676	DH	Dirck Harlees 1795
	Rochus Jacobs Hoppestein, 1680	P	**The Porcelain Dish** Johannes Pennis 1759
R $		P.	
AK	c. 1700	P	
G·V·S	Geertruy Verstelle, 1764	C PS	
G·V·S		Duyn	Johannes van Duyn, 1764
	The Peacock 1651 —— = D. Pauw		**The Roman** c. 1670 ——
DAN			Imitations of Chinese marks
DAW 4/2			
IDM	Jacobus de Milde 1759		
jD·	**The Pole** = Inde Dessel	M: P.V·M	Petrus van Marum, 1759
	The Porcelain Axe 1679	RR	Renier Hey, 1697
B	Justus Brouwer 1759	VK	Johannes van der Kloot Jansz, 1764

Mark.	Description.	Mark.	Description.
Roos ❀ ❀ ❀	**The Rose** 1675		**The Three Ash-barrels** Gerrit Pietersz Kam, 1674 *De drie Aschtonnen*
D ♡ D	Dirck van der Does, 1759	a ꝫ stonne	
✳	**The Star** 1690	HV'hvorn HvH	Hendrick van Hoorn, 1759
H	Damis Hofdick 1705		
CB	Cornelis de Berg, 1720		**The Three Bells**
✶		WD	Willem van der Does, 1764
l Aalmis	Aalnis, 1720 (also at Rotterdam)	VK.	**The Three Bottles** Willem Kool 1697
iB	Justus de Berg 1759	Ṛ	**The Three Porcelain Bottles** Jacobus Pynacker 1672
A·K·	Albertus Kiell 1764	Ṙ	Hugo Brouwer 1764
L P Kan	**The Ewer** or (*Lampet kan*) taken by Gerrit Brouwer, 1759	HB	
lpk		Z·DEX.	**The Three Tuns** Zacharias Dextra 1720
CPK		W·V·B	**The Two Savages** Willem van Beck 1764
l jet Kan		Æ	
Cl VDkeelm	Abraham van der Keel, 1780	Æ	**The Two Wherries** Anthony Pennis 1759

Mark.	Description.	Mark.	Description.
	Miscellaneous	A·I·	Arij Jansz, 1658
TOME ƧWA	Thomas Jansz 1590-1611	F·V·FRYTOM	Frederick van Frytom, 1658
16 ₵⊣ 34	Gerrit Hermansz 1614 ——	IG	Jan Groenlant 1660
C	Cornelis Cornelisz, 1628	ḥ	Jan Ariensz van Hammen, 1661
P	Pieter van Kessel	(J&K)	Jan Jansz Culick (or Kulick), 1662
LG	Lambrecht Ghisbrechts, 1640	k	Johannes Kruyck 1662
Junius $\frac{6}{16}$ 1657	Isaack Junius 1640	1:G $\overline{2\ 2\frac{1}{2}}$	Jacob Cornelisz (van der Burgh) 1662
AK	Aelbrecht de Keiser, 1642, and Adrianus Koex of The Alpha	RP AP	Augesteyn Reygens (or Reygensberg) 1663
AK	Ghisbrecht Lambrechtse Kruyk, 1645 (who worked ? at The Alpha)	AR	
K	,,	$\frac{WK}{4}$	Willem Kleftijus 1663
G	,,		
K		IDW	Jan de Weert 1663
LH	Jan Gerrits van der Hoeve 1649	ES	Johannes Mesch 1667
G		R	Pieter Gerritsz Kam, 1667
Ⓐ	Q. Aldersz Kleijnoven, 1655	CK	Cornelis Albrechtsz de Keizer, 1668
IVK	Jeronimus Pietersz van Kessel, 1655	₳	The same combined with Adrien Pynacker

MARK.	DESCRIPTION.	MARK.	DESCRIPTION.
P	**Miscellaneous** Jan Pietersz 1668	§§	Sixtius van der Sand, 1705
F	Flyt. M. Byclok 1669	GAAL	Johannes Gaal, 1707
AT	Arij Jansz van der Meer, 1671		
L K	Lucas Pietersz van Kessel, 1675	IG	
D: V:schii	Dirck Jansz van Schie, 1679	J:C	(MVB=Math : van der Bogaert 1714)
iG	Johannes Groen, 1683	Leonardus VA	Leonard van Amsterdam, 1721
R		P.V.D:S	Paulus van der Stroom, 1725
AK	Adriaen Pynacker, 1690	J.Heß. F.	Frederick van Hesse, 1730
AK		HS R	
P	Pieter Poulisse 1690		
ivW	Johannes van der Wal, 1691	P Vizeer	Piet Vizeer, 1752
LV	Lucas van Dale, 1692		
iB	Jan van der Buergen (or Verburg), 1693	G Verhuast	1760
jvB		IVPsC	Jan van Putten and Co., 1830. Combined the Three Bells, Claw and Rose factories
CW	Cornelis Witsenburg, 1696		**Arnhem**
I: Baan	J. Baan c. 1698. (Also AB in monogram for A. C. Brouwer 1699)		c. 1780 H. van Laun

Mark.	Description.	Mark.	Description.
	Holland Late 17th cent. on red ware	$M:oL:=$	**Oude Loosdrecht** c. 1772-1782
	,,	$M:OL.$	Moll, the founder h. p. Inc., p. in blue and red
	Weesp 1764-71 h. p. p. in blue	*A. Lafon de Comp* *à Amsterdam*	**Amsterdam** 1810 h. p.
	p. in blue and red	*F. L. S.* *A Rotterdam* *WcM:1812*	? Painted only at Rotterdam
	? Luxemburg Late 18th cent. h. p. p. in lilac		**Tournay** 1750-99 Porcelain, s. p. A tower, arms of the town
	The Hague Arms of the town 1775-86 h. p. p. in blue		Early mark p. in red, gold, and blue
	,, p. in red		
	Oude Amstel 1782-c. 1800 h. p.		Arms of Peterinck (founder of the factory) 1769-97 p. in blue and gold
Amstel	p. in blue		I D ? initials of the painter Duvivier
	A. Dareuber, director		Tournay faïence

MARK.	DESCRIPTION.	MARK.	DESCRIPTION.
L. cretté *Bruxelles*	**Brussels** Late 18th cent. Rue d'Aremberg 1791-1813 Porcelain, h.p. L. Cretté. p. in red.	C̄C̄C̄ C͞P	**Tervueren** 1767-81 Manufactory of Prince Charles of Lorraine in the Castle of Tervueren. Faïence
L.c		I M	**Malines** 18th cent.
B	**Etterbeek** 1775-1803	ꭅ	**Bruges** *Briquet* from the arms of the town 18th cent.
👑	Brussels Montplaisir 1784-91 p. in blue		
B		ꟼP ꟼꟼ	H. Pulinx
WB	Faïence, 1705. Witsenburg and Mombaers.	④ (·BOCH·A·LUXEMBOURG·)	**Luxemburg** (Septfontaines) Boch brothers 1767 onwards Earthenware
BRUSSEL			
MB	Ph. Mombaers 1724 ——	Ɫ₿ X̶R	,,
👑	,,	B	,,
C.B ∴		Φ Bx M:Q λ	,,
👑	,,		
CꟼP		(BLC)	**Ardenne** B. Lammens and Co. Early 19th cent. Earthenware
:B: / 5	,,		
⚱ ·L ⎮ G·	**Liège** 18th cent.	Æ.W.	A. van der Waert

MARK.	DESCRIPTION.	MARK.	DESCRIPTION.
Herreböe ̄R	**Herreböe** (Norway) 1750-63 Faïence	*H* $\frac{15}{12}$ 60 *Dr* *R' 81* 71 *Oon*	**Rörstrand** (Stockholm) 1726-83
Joseph Large			
HB H.			**Marieberg** 1758-c. 1788 Faïence
H AR,			
N⁰3		MB ̄Sten	
🐝	**Gudumlund** Wolfsen and Sons 1805	͝ ͝ ̄MB.	
Stockholm $\frac{12}{2}$ ⅔!	**Stockholm** Rörstrand 1726-83 Faïence	⚓S	**Gustafsberg** Godenius, 1827 onwards
Stuck $\frac{12}{3}$ 55		*F.5*	**Copenhagen** Porcelain s.p. 1760-65 Cypher of Frederick V. in gold and blue. 1772 onwards h.p. The mark represents the Three Belts. p. in blue
Rörstrand		≋	
Rör $\cancel{H}\frac{29}{6}$ 67 *H*		✠	? Copenhagen. p. in blue
R — C:E		B.& G	Bing and Grondahl 1853 onwards

Mark.	Description.	Mark.	Description.
MB	**Marieberg** 1758-89 Porcelain, s.p. 1766-69. Inc.		**St. Petersburg** porcelain, h.p. c. 1745 onwards. The double eagle occurs in a wreath
MB *T*	H.p. The Three crowns from the arms of Sweden and initials of directors or artists F. S. etc., 1778-82 p. in blue.	**ЕП**	Royal cyphers. p. in blue. Catherine II. 1762-96
		П:К 2	Pridvornie Cortoia (Imperial Court)
A	on a hybrid porcelain	*Придворе*	*Pridvornie* = belonging to the imperial court
I	The three crowns and emblem of the house of Vasa. p. in pink	**П**	Paul (1796-1801)
КІЕВЬ	**Russia** Kieff pottery	**А** **Нс**	Alexander I. (1801-25) Nicolas I. (1825-55)
		АП	Alexander II. 1855-81
	Stawsk 1843-7 Pottery	**Н** II	Nicolas II. 1894 ——
I.R		**ГАРДНЕРZ**	**Moscow** 1780 —— h.p.
Baranŭʀka	**Baranowka** in Volhynia Porcelain, h.p. p. in sepia	**C** **A**	Gardner pr. in red
Korʒɛc 9	**Korzec** Porcelain, h.p. Early 19th cent. p. in red		

Mark.	Description.	Mark.	Description.
ПОПОВЫ	**Moscow** H.p. porcelain A. Popoff Early 19th cent. P. in blue Gospodina factory :	HH G	**Winterthur** Hans Heinrich Graf, 1662
АП		KE DF	? Ehrhardt
ФГ ГУЛИНА	Gulena, potter c. 1850	H. E. A. M. I. T. 1647	(Stove tile makers)
		D M	
ВРАТЬЕВЪ	Brothers Korniloff, St. Petersburg 1827 ——	*Daniel Hafner Steckborn*	**Steckborn** 1790
КОРНИЛОВЫХЪ		E. I. F.	**Bern** Früting, 1772
(Заводъ С.Т.КУЗНЕЦОВА 83 Rиa 5)	,,	H. K. R. 1705	
		Simon Jean Renaud fecit, 1769	**Neuchâtel**
(crossed marks)	**Mezer** Early 19th cent.	*Lutri 1602*	**Vaud** Lautry
Tomaszow Mezer		J5-92 W	**Zurich** Pottery Caspar Meyer
L. P. 1620	**Winterthur** (Switzerland) Ludwig Pfau	M	,,
D. P. 1636	David Pfau	*Baltus Meyer 1602*	
A. P. 1686	Abraham Pfau	*Heinrich Stadler*	1670
A. B. 1638	(Signatures, chiefly on stove tiles)	D. S.	David Sulzer
S. M. S. 1647		*Hans Ulrich Hegner*	1656
H. P. Z		*Hans Jacob DA. KER*	1724
B. E		*Hoffmann pinxit*	1757
		Z B/Z	Zurich Faïence 1763-1791

MARK.	DESCRIPTION.	MARK.	DESCRIPTION.
S.O. $\frac{1707}{40}$ H.C.W.	**? Solothurn** Pottery	$\dot{H}$ H $VC46$ $\dot{H}Z$ H $\dagger 522$	**Strassburg** and **Hagenau** Joseph Hannong Porcelain, h.p. 1760-80. p. in blue
⚓ (anchor)	**(Poppelsdorf** near Bonn 18th cent. M. Wessel)		
Schaphuysen Gerrit Evers	**Schaffhausen** c. 1795 Slip ware	$\dot{W}$ PW	? Strassburg Faïence
Paulus Hammekers	c. 1743 **Zurich** porcelain	$\overset{W}{T}$	**Niderwiller** Beyerlé; faïence 1754; porcelain h.p. 1765-
$\underset{..}{Z}$ ZR	(1763-1791) s.p. at first afterwards h.p. p. in blue	$\mathcal{M}$	
(fish)	**Nyon** 1781-1813 Arms of the town p. in blue	$\mathcal{CV}$	Comte de Custine 1780-1801
D	D =? Dortu	$\mathcal{X}$ $\overset{.}{\mathcal{X}}$ $\mathcal{L}$	
Gide	1789 Gide, painter	$\overset{\mathcal{W}}{\mathcal{X}}$	
$\mathcal{PFr\&C}$ (fish)	Pfluger frères & Co.	$\mathcal{C}$	Claude François Lanfrey, manager to 1801, and proprietor to 1827
	Strassburg Ch. Hannong (1710-39) Faïence and porcelain	NIDERVILLER *Le Mire Ainé*	18th cent. Lemire, modeller
CH ch	H.p. 1721-55. p. in blue	*N Nider*	since 1794
H $\mathcal{IK}$ $H\cdot$ Q		*Niderwiller*	
$\mathcal{M}$ $\mathcal{G}$	Paul Hannong 1739-54	CYFFLE A LUNEVILLE S	**Lunéville** (1731 onwards) Cyfllé, modeller b. 1724, † 1806. pottery

Mark.	Description.	Mark.	Description
TERRE DE LORRAINE *Leopold*	**Lunéville** (1731 ——) Cefflé's terracottas	S & G W S & S S & Co G. G.	**Bohemia, etc.** "Siderolith" ware mid. 19th cent.
T D L T / AB T	= Terre de Lorraine **Toul** c. 1790 Earthenware Bayard at Toul	BARUCH	**Ratibor** cream ware
K. et G. LUNÉVILLE	Keller and Guérin late 18th cent.		**Saargemünd** (Sarreguemines) 1775 —— Pot. and porcelain
✳ 8 ✳ f	**Strassburg** faïence early marks	U & C	Utzschneider & Co.
† S x		Ll & Cⁱᵉ	

FRANCE

IT is not yet definitely settled where the celebrated "Henri II. ware" was made. Formerly it was supposed to have been made at the Castle of Oiron, near Thouars, but it is now more generally assigned to the neighbouring village of Porchaire. This ware is very rare and remarkable. It is a fine, glazed earthenware of ivory colour, with stamped patterns, like those on contemporary book-bindings, inlaid with darker clays, and occasionally touched with colour. The shapes are carefully and elaborately moulded ; and the occurrence of the royal arms, and the cyphers of Henri II. and Diane de Poitiers attest the royal appreciation of the ware. Commoner lead-glazed earthenwares were made from early times at Beauvais, and in the neighbourhood of Saintes, but they are rarely marked. Nor has any marked example of undisputed Palissy ware been found. Bernard Palissy, the most renowned of French potters, was born about 1510 near Saintes, and by extraordinary patience and all-sacrificing industry succeeded in making the peculiar type of pottery associated forever with his name. It is a fine dense pottery with rich lead-glaze mottled or splashed with blue, green, purple, and yellow : most of the pieces are enriched with relief designs, but perhaps the most characteristic are the rustic dishes with accurately moulded shells, lizards, eels, and aquatic creatures in relief and coloured after nature. Palissy is said to have died in the Bastille about 1592. His sons continued the work, and among his other followers were several potters at Avon, near Fontainebleau, including Barthélemy de Blémont, to whom the mark B B (p. 59) is attributed. Palissy ware has been frequently copied, Pull of Paris, about 1850, being particularly successful in this work.

In the seventeenth and eighteenth centuries the French potters devoted themselves to the manufacture of tin-enamelled faïence, first in imitation of Italian maiolica, and afterwards of Dutch delft. The processes employed were essentially the same as those described on page 1 in connection with the Italian ware. Indeed the art was introduced into the south of France by Italian potters at the end of the sixteenth century, and the early wares of Lyons and Nevers are purely Italian in style. Among the many forms of decoration adopted on French faïence five distinct schools are observable :—(1) The Italian. (2) The Persian style adopted at Nevers for a short period in the seventeenth century; it consisted of white floral ornament on a deep blue ground. (3) The Rouen school, characterised first by the use of scalloped borders and embroidery patterns, recalling lace work, and afterwards by a commoner decoration, in which a cornucopia is the central motive. (4) Delicate arabesques with Chinese figures and interlacings, after the designs of Berain, adopted at Moustiers early in the eighteenth century. (5) Enamelled bouquets of flowers and landscapes in scroll-edged panels, after the manner of the porcelain painters, introduced at Strassburg, and largely developed at Marseilles and elsewhere in the eighteenth century. About 1780 " cream-colour " and other English forms of fine earthenware threatened to oust the national faïence, and attempts were made to produce the English types of earthenware, notably at Douai and Creil. The marks on French faïence are mostly painted in blue, sometimes in colours.

FRENCH PORCELAIN

FRANCE was the home of soft-paste porcelain. At the end of the seventeenth century this ware was successfully made, first at Rouen, then at St. Cloud, and a few years later it was made at Lille, Mennecy, and Chantilly. The perfection of soft paste was reached at Vincennes and Sèvres between the years 1740-70. The true soft-paste largely consists of a glassy composition or frit mixed with sand and marl or pipe-clay and other ingredients and is coated with a luscious lead-glaze of creamy tone. The body is tender enough to be easily scratched with a steel point, and the glaze is so soft that the enamels painted upon it sink in and become incorporated in the moderate heat of the enamelling kiln. The ware is very beautiful, but unsuited for household usage. About 1768 the manufacture of true or hard-paste porcelain from natural clays and rocks was introduced at Sèvres, and very soon superseded the soft-paste there and elsewhere in France. It was made in large quantities in Paris from about 1770 to the end of the century, but since then the chief centre of production has been Limoges. Figures and groups in "biscuit" or unglazed porcelain were made in both hard and soft paste. These are usually marked by incising in the raw body, whereas the glazed wares are marked by painting in under-glaze blue, over-glaze red, and other colours or gilding, and on the modern wares by printing chiefly in red.

EARLY FRENCH EARTHENWARES

MARK.	DESCRIPTION.	MARK.	DESCRIPTION.
	Saint Porchaire 16th century. Formerly attributed to Oiron. The ware is commonly called "Henri II. ware." The crescents refer to Diane de Poictiers		**Beauvais** 16th cent.
	Cypher of Henri II. and Diane de Poictiers		**Saintes** 16th cent. ? François Briot, Paris ? Barthélemy de Blémont at **Avon** c. 1580 Mark of a follower of Palissy

MARK.	DESCRIPTION.	MARK.	DESCRIPTION.
Lyon	**Lyons** Combe's pottery c. 1740	*3: Cuſtodeſſ*	**Nevers** J. Custode 17th cent.
Gf *C. C.*		H·B 1689.	H. Borne
I. P. S.	? Patras c. 1750	DLF	Denis Lefèbvre 1636
Patras		F. R	François Rodrique early 18th cent.
J. B. Revol	c. 1753	S	Jacques Seigne 1726
Pierre Marie Mongis *Rogé*	c. 1750	L ⊗	
Bondino	And others in 18th cent.	N ⊗	? Nicolas Viode c. 1700
	Nevers late 16th cent. Dominique Conrade	P	
		H.S.R	Signoret 1870
		R	T. Ristori 1850
	Jacques Bourdu at the Conrade factory early 17th cent.		
	? J. Boulard	*faicta Rouen* 1647	**Rouen**

MARK.	DESCRIPTION.	MARK.	DESCRIPTION.
Mrs Guillibeaux	**Rouen** (1644-c. 1800) Guillebaud 1722 ———	*gardin*	**Rouen** 1782
C.lle			P. Omonz
✝ *GllS*		*1790*	
Borne Pinxit		*faik Bar Biene o mony*	
Anno 1738		*J. Guillaume*	
•Ⓑ• *1736*	Claude Borne	W....·.	? Le Vavasseur
I PERDV	1734		
dieul	1756 ———		
Ꝛ.			
Fossé	Veuve Fossé c. 1757		
Hilaire	1759		
Mallet	c. 1756		
S A S	1743-94	4c. P.	And other numbers (see p. 62)
vauasseur a Rouan	Le Vavasseur 1743-1800	4 ⊹.	
d R		6	
V R		I B	

(see p. 62)

A

A

A

AB

A (monogram)

AR

BB

BD

B

B (monogram)

B2H

B31B

B·L

C Cb

C Ṅ

C1B

CO

·C·S·

DA
1708

B

D 4

DD

7

Dg

DM

DP

E

F

f

FB

4

fⁿB

F⁶B

B

ff

R

fR

G·f·
·f·

G·3

GA

GÆ

Eß

Gha

GIB

GL

GMⅉ2

GRD2

GS2

HB

hJ1732

HJ
4

HVXX

HR

B (monogram)

IB10

IVLR
1734

LA

LC
1734

LD

Lſ

L
I

Lm

M

M·D·

M

MIIⱢ

MR

nH

NIB

P3

MP

Pa

PÆ

PB

PD

Pn

PX

R

RD

S

SG

T

T◊B

TP
1776

VD

VLI

VL
2

VL
N

XBC

A number of
marks prob-
ably of
painters
from c. 1750
onwards.

Numbers
also occur
referring to
the value of
the ware.

Single letters
also occur on
ware made in
two pieces
(*e.g.* sugar-
castors) to
identify the
parts.

MARK.	DESCRIPTION.	MARK.	DESCRIPTION.
SₑT	**St. Cloud** c. 1670 onwards	ROUY	**Rouy** 1790-c. 1850
S·C T	T initial of Trou c. 1710	B	**Lille** J. Boussemart (1729-1802)
S ·S· S+	**Sinceny** 1734-1864	B	
Sincheny· 8ᵐᵉ D		B	J. F. Boussemart (Lille or St. Amand)
S ⁺C⁺		F B	
·S·C·ÿ S		C :B.M C B M	Painter's mark
L·JLC. pinxit joseph le cerf 1776		D	? Dorez
B·T	Bertrand	L LL	
B	Joseph Bedeau	N·A· DOREZ 1748	Dorez (1720-50) Faïence and porcelain
S·A ·C·S·		P	? Lille
⊕	Pierre Jeannot	B ✳P	Lefèbvre et Petit
L·M	L. Malériat	V ✳	
Gh	Ghäil		

Mark.	Description.	Mark.	Description.
	Valenciennes F. L. Dorez Early 18th cent.	*G. viry f. a Moustiers chez Clérissy* 1711	**Moustiers** 1679-1852 Clérissy's factory 1679-1748
		F. V. F.	François Viry fecit c. 1685
	Picard's factory c. 1756	G. V. F.	Gaspard Viry fecit
	Saint-Amand-les-Eaux 18th cent. marks of Pierre Fauquez	*Vf Fe*	? Fouque successor of Clérissy
		ff. Ef	
			Fouque and Pelloquin 1749-
		EB	Jean Étienne Baron, c. 1750
		M . C	
		M . C A 1756	
		J . A *g*	
		f^d F^d	? Ferraud
	Painter † 1815	*Soliua*	Painters at Clérissy's 18th cent. See also Alcora (p. 90)
		Miguel Vilax	
	Dijon 1669-1854	*ca*	
		Fo Grangel	
		CROS	

Mark.	Description.	Mark.	Description.
	Olerys, a painter at Clérissy's factory, started a pottery in 1738. The monogram of O L indicates his work. His factory lasted till 1749, his partner being Laugier. After 1749 he worked as a painter again till 1783.		**Moustiers** Guichard c. 1763
			Varages c. 1750 ——
			Tavernes c. 1760
			G. for Gaze
			Marseilles A. Clérissy, 1697
	? Ferraud		? Savy, 1749- The fleur-de-lys after 1777
	Late 18th cent. ? Achard		J. G. Robert c. 1750-93
	P. Fournier		Veuve Perrin c. 1760
			Antoine Bonnefoy
			J. Fauchier
	1778		Jacques Borelli (see p. 21) 1781

Mark.	Description.	Mark.	Description.
Mouchard	**Montauban** (1720-1820) Mouchard, 1792	P · B · C ·	**Nimes** Plautier Boncoirant & Co. 19th cent.
M. Mat.		MB	**La Rochelle** last half of the 18th cent.
FAZ 1778 D·L·S	D. Lestrade	*B* *B*	
L *QL*	Lapierre Lapierre et Quinquiry c. 1780	*B*	
Clermond fᵈ m	**Clermont-Ferrand** 1734	*E* *P* *C*	? Pouhet Colin or Chaux
Samadet	**Samadet** 1732	*B*	1783
St. ardus Pichon f	**Ardus** 1736 —— Pichon, c. 1752	-J*R-	Jean Roland 1780
D	Dupré, c. 1740	MR	= Manufacture La Rochelle
(DE MONTPELLIER Fᵍ & cᵉ I.V.)	**Montpellier** Le Voulant 18th cent.	MÆRAN	**Marans** 1740-56
		R	
Laurens Basso A Toulouza	**Toulouse** 1756	*M*	**Sceaux** c. 1750-1813 S P = Sceaux Penthièvre. The anchor refers to the Duc de P. high admiral of France
NISMES, 1581	**Nimes**	S P ⚓ ⚓	

MARK.	DESCRIPTION.	MARK.	DESCRIPTION.
AP j	**Aprey** 1744- Jarry, painter, and others	**T**	**Rennes** Tortia
A·v.		*Pierre Le Duc*	1834
P·A		*Morice (Jean)*	1834
AP G		*I·R·PAIvadeAV.* *1643*	**Nantes**
hirel de choisy pencit	**Rennes** H. de Choisy 1767	*R*	**? Apt** 18th cent.
H·C **C·** **C·**		*JMB*	**Bordeaux** Vieillard & Co. 19th cent.
CHOISY FT		*L^R*	Lahens and Rateau
P *Bourgouin* *1776*	J. B. A. Bourgouin	**A MORREIN** *Poitiers*	**Poitiers** 1752
pinxit baron a rennes	Baron 1772	*F·F*	Félix Faucon
Michel Derennes	1771	**PC** **C**	**Quimper** (1690-c. 1800)
fait a Rennes Rue Hue	1769	*Q Z*	Pierre Caussy 1749-82
Luc Bouchereau	1780		A. de la Hubeaudière 1782-
Raymond			

MARK.	DESCRIPTION.	MARK.	DESCRIPTION.
H	**St. Omer** 1751-90	DOUAI	**Douai** 1780-1820 Leigh & Co. Cream ware in English style
N			
P P		*4 B 1 B*	
R	**Aire** 1780 ——	*Leigh & Cie*	
R k	? Prudhomme	*W i x*	
p	**Vron** late 18th cent. Verlingue	*I ⟨shield⟩ S*	Houzé, de l'Aulnoit & Co. 1784 followed by Halsfort in 1788
W			
Jankm J.		D. C. B R A.	
J × Jamart 1696	? Vron	R.	
Fait à Desvres, 1778	**Desvres**	HALSFORT	
J. van der Plas		BLONDEL	
D P *4 P*	Dupré-Poulaine 1732 ——	*Martin Damman*	1799-1803 **Castillon** late 18th cent.
G y		*Castilhon*	**Épinal** 1760 ——
h)		EPINAL	**Premières** J. Lavalle 1783 ——
		J L S. PAUL	**St. Paul** 18th and 19th cent.

Mark.	Description.	Mark.	Description.
CREIL	**Creil** 1794 —— Cream ware		**Bourg la Reine** Veuve Laurier et fils. Rebus of Chapelet, painter. 19th cent.
PARIS	Monogram of Stone, Coquerel and Legros, transfer-printers c. 1830		
Angoulême anno, 1770	**Angoulême**		**Tours d'Aigues** 18th cent.
	Casamène Early 19th cent. (near Bebançon)		c. 1753
		Bergerac	**Bergerac**
CAMBRAY	**Cambray**		**Renac**
EPERNAY	**Epernay** 17th and 18th cent.		18th cent.
JEAN GAUTIER	**Vauvert** (near Nimes) c. 1736		**Courcelles** (Maine), c. 1783
fait a Martres	**Martres** 1775	*Courcelles*	**Saint Longe** Late 18th cent.
+ ‖G‖	**Goult** 1740 ——	*Saint Longe*	**Ligron** 1787. Copy of Palissy ware
a Moulins	**Moulins** 18th cent.	*Lacouves Gallet de Ligron*	
Chollet fecit de Moulain	1742		**Orleans** 1753 ——
BlaR	**Bourg la Reine**	T3UH	
BR OP	18th cent.	*Forges*	**Forges les Eaux** 18th cent. imp.

MARK.	DESCRIPTION.	MARK.	DESCRIPTION.
D V	? **Mennecy** or Rouen 18th cent.	ℒ	**Tours** Landais 19th cent. Style of Palissy
Claude Pelisie 1726	**Val Sous Meudon**		
M. Sansont 1738		*L'italienne*	near Beauvais late 18th cent.
d' Entoine d'engle fontaine	**Englefontaine**		**Batignolles** 19th cent. Lesorre
CHANTILLY	**Chantilly** 18th cent.		
		(RUBELLES S & M)	**Rubelles** (Seine et Marne) 1836-58
	M. Aaron 1845 —— porcelain	A. D. T.	Baron de Tremble 1856 ——
M A	**Mathaux** (Champagne) 1751-1800	*Manufacture de Saint Clément*	**Saint Clément** 1757 ——
M	**Ognes** (Aisne), 1748-82	GALLE NANCY	19th cent.
C H			
A Limoges 1741	**Limoges**	*Geoffroi*	**Gien** 19th cent.
Fait a tours 1782	**Tours**	(GIEN)	Geoffroi pr. and imp.
LOVIS LIAVTE		(G BAYEUX)	**Bayeux** 1810 —— porcelain
avisseau a tour	Avisseau c. 1855	*Saint Amans*	**Lamarque** 1835-58
ℳ	,, imitations of Palissy ware	3 P	**Meudon** 18th cent.

Mark.	Description.	Mark.	Description.
SEVRES	**Sévres** late 18th cent. Lambert, Levasseur, Clavareau c. 1806- **Voisinlieu** initials of J. Ziegler (in a double quartrefoil). 19th cent. imp.	*Vve. Dumas*	**Paris** 1834-62
J·Z		PULL	Pull, c. 1850 Style of Palissy
W		TD	Th. Deck 1859 ——
Pajou, 1787	**Paris** terracotta	B V	V. Barbizet 1850 —— Style of Palissy
Claude Remey	,, C. Remey 1817	H	**Vincennes** 1767-71 Hannong : faïence
OLLIVIER A PARIS	Rue Roquette late 18th cent.	B	
Masson	formerly Olivier 19th cent.	X	
j P.	J. Petit, at Belleville 1770 —— Porcelain	DENUELLE	**Paris** h.p. porcelain c. 1800 Rue de Crussol
C	M. Gille 1845 —— Porcelain biscuit imp.	*Deroche*	
PASCAL	F. M. Pascal	RIBOUET	Rue de la Paix (agent)
MP	c. 1850 ——	*Guerin*	
H	J. Devers 19th cent.	H L	

Mark.	Description.	Mark.	Description.
A P *	**Rouen** Poterat late 17th cent. s.p.	VALENCIEN	**Valenciennes** 1785-97 h.p.
(sun mark)	**Saint Cloud** late 17th cent. —— c. 1773 s.p. p. in blue	*L*	Fauquez and Vannier
4 S·C T	Trou 1712 —— p. in blue and inc.	*LL*	Fauquet and Lamoninary. p. in blue
C M. 12 +. B.B.	p. in blue	*LL* *LL*	
ℓL+ ✝I✝		*L* *LL*	p. in red
S· P. E.		(horn mark)	**Chantilly** 1725-89 s.p.
F+ M+		(horn mark)	p. in red or gold
D AD	**Lille** 1711 —— s.p. Dorez. p. in blue	(horn mark)	
ℓ. LL		(horn marks)	
(dolphin mark)	Leperre Durot 1784 h.p. under patronage of the Dauphin	Chantilly	
fait par Lebrun à Lille	p. in black	.D·V· 2 DV	**Mennecy** Duc de Villeroy 1735-73 s.p.
Lillw W		D,Vf	p. in blue or inc.
		DC,O	Crépy-en-Valois

Mark.	Description.	Mark.	Description.
	Bourg-la-Reine 1774-89 s.p. inc.		**Orléans** 1753-70 Soft paste
	? Bourg-la-Reine		1770 —— hard paste. p. in blue
	Sceaux 1749 —— s.p. inc.		Inc.
	p. in blue		Bourdon c. 1788 G = ? Gérault
	Under patronage of the High Admiral, Duc de Penthièvre. Hence the anchor and S. P. = (Sceaux Penthièvre)		1790-1811
	Arras c. 1782-88 s.p. p. in blue		Le Brun 1808-11
	Etiolles 1768 —— Pellevé s.p. and h.p. inc.		**Bordeaux** 1770 —— Verneuille **Boisette** 1778. h.p. p. in blue
	Monnier 1786 ——		**Limoges** h.p. 1783 —— Grellet (1783-88)
	Marseilles J. G. Robert c. 1777 h.p. p. in blue		? Alluaud 1788 ——

Mark.	Description.	Mark.	Description.
CAEN *Le francois à Caen*	**Caen** 1798-1808. h.p. st. in red	M A P	**Paris** h.p. *Faubourg St. Antoine* 1773 —— Morel
	Boulogne Haffringue 19th cent. h.p.		*Fabrique de la Courtille* 1773 —— Locré.
	St. Amand- les-Eaux 19th cent. h.p. and s.p.		with letters R, X, W, H, etc. inc.
	Montreuil 19th cent. h.p.		Locré and Russinger 1784-94
	Choisy-le-Roy c. 1780 h.p. pr.	L et R P. R	'' Pouyat and Russinger c. 1800 ——
	Paris h.p. Le Comte de Brancas Lauraguais c. 1758. *Faubourg St. Lazare* 1769-1810. Mark of P.A. Hannong 1772-75. Cypher of Charles Philippe Comte d'Artois, patron. p. in gold	L L C·H G. Pf P CG	*Rue de Reuilly* Lassia 1774-c. 1800 Chanon *Rue du Petit Carousel* 1775 ——

MARK.	DESCRIPTION.	MARK.	DESCRIPTION.
	Paris h.p. *Clignancourt*, 1775-c. 1790 founded by P. Deruelle under the patronage of Monsieur, the King's eldest brother. p. in blue, gold, and red	*Dibl.*	**Paris** h.p. *Rue de Bondy.* p. in blue Monogram of G. A.
Moitte M	De Moitte who succeeded Deruelle	N... a Paris	*Rue de Popin-court*, 1780 —— Bought by Nast in 1783
GROSSE L'ISLE SAINT DENIS	*L'isle Saint Denis* c. 1780	nast a paris NAST	In gold
	Fabrique de la Reine, *Rue Thiroux*, 1778 —— p. in blue and red : founded by Leboeuf. Cypher of Queen Marie Antoinette. Managed by Guy and Housel after the Revolution	DARTE M Royal	M. Darté fl. 1812
A. Housel			*Pont-aux-Choux* 1784-c. 1806 Cypher of Louis Philippe, the patron, and monogram MJ of the Director
Gh Rue Thirou a Paris.			Monogram of J. B. Outrequin de Montarcy 1786 ——
MANUFRE *de Mer le Duc d'Angouleme* MANUFRE *de MM Guerhard et Dihl à Paris*	*Rue de Bondy*, founded in 1780 by Guerhard and Dihl under the patronage of the Duc d'Angoulême. st. in red	B Potter 42 P B ·E B	*Rue de Crussol*, 1789, founded by Potter, an Englishman p. in blue

MARK.	DESCRIPTION.	MARK.	DESCRIPTION.
FLEURY	**La Seinie** c. 1774-94 h. p. (near Limoges) **Paris** h. p. St. Denis late 18th cent.		**Paris** h. p. Feuillet 19th cent.
PONTEINX	**Ponteinx** 1790-c. 1810 (Landes) **Paris** h. p. *Gros Caillou.* J. L. Broillet 1762-69 A. Lamarre 1773-		*Belleville.* Jacob Petit 1790 onwards. p. in blue **Vincennes** h. p. cypher of the patron Louis Philippe, Duc de Chartres, 1767-86
F. D. HONORÉ	*Bould St. Antoine* 1785		
F. M. HONORÉ			Hannong
R. F. DAGOTY			? Hannong and Lemaire. p. in blue
DAGOTY ET HONORÉ			
FABRIQUE DE L'IMPERATRICE P. L. DAGOTY	*Boulᵈ Poissonière* 1780		
le Bon halley I	? Paris. In gold		
Monginot	20 *Boulevard des Italiens*	TANAY	**Vincennes** s. p. (1740-56) ? painter's name c. 1750. p. in red. Incised on Vincennes porcelain, 1753
C. H. PILLIVUYT *Manufacture de Foëscy*	Pillivuyt & Co. 1817- also at Foëscy		
Schoelcher	*Faubourg St. Lazare* early 19th cent.		

MARK.	DESCRIPTION.	MARK.	DESCRIPTION.
	Sèvres		**Sèvres**
F	inc. marks on biscuit porcelain. Fernex or Falconet	*Brachard ainé*	1823
M·G.		S.6	1806 initials of repairer
B	Brachard father and son	h·B	
Bon	? Bourdus		**Vincennes** (1740-56) soft paste. p. in blue
JS	Liance		
RL	? Robert le Lorrain		
⟨→⟩	Le Riche	A	1753
LR			**Sèvres** (1756 onwards) 1756. soft paste made exclusively till 1769, and as well as hard paste till c. 1804; after which hard paste almost entirely.
Pajou	1771	D	
T	? Tristan, 1769		1777. p. in blue
P	? Perrotin, 1774	AA	
BO			
BD		U (crowned)	1772 on hard paste porcelain from 1769
A.B 6 n F	Alexandre Brachard		

Letters, marks, and numbers indicating the year in which Vincennes and Sèvres porcelain was decorated.

A denotes the year 1753	AA denotes the year 1778	T9 denotes the
B ,, ,, 1754	BB ,, ,, 1779	IX year 1801
C ,, ,, 1755	CC ,, ,, 1780	X ,, X ,, 1802
D ,, ,, 1756	DD ,, ,, 1781	11 ,, XI ,, 1803
E ,, ,, 1757	EE ,, ,, 1782	÷ ,, XII ,, 1804
F ,, ,, 1758	FF ,, ,, 1783	–‖– ,, XIII ,, 1805
G ,, ,, 1759	GG ,, ,, 1784	⊥ ,, XIV ,, 1806
H ,, ,, 1760	HH ,, ,, 1785	7 denotes the year 1807
I ,, ,, 1761	II ,, ,, 1786	8 ,, ,, 1808
J ,, ,, 1762	JJ ,, ,, 1787	9 ,, ,, 1809
K ,, ,, 1763	KK ,, ,, 1788	10 ,, ,, 1810
L ,, ,, 1764	LL ,, ,, 1789	oz ,, ,, 1811
M ,, ,, 1765	MM ,, ,, 1790	dz ,, ,, 1812
N ,, ,, 1766	NN ,, ,, 1791	tz ,, ,, 1813
O ,, ,, 1767	OO ,, ,, 1792	qz ,, ,, 1814
P ,, ,, 1768	PP[2] ,, ,, 1793	qn ,, ,, 1815
Q[1] ,, ,, 1769		sz ,, ,, 1816
R ,, ,, 1770		ds ,, ,, 1817
S ,, ,, 1771		
T ,, ,, 1772	Letters denoting the year	From 1818-1834 the year
U ,, ,, 1773	fell into disuse during the	was indicated by the last
V ,, ,, 1774	time of the Revolution,	two figures of the date, e.g.
X ,, ,, 1775	and between 1793-1800	18 denotes 1818
Y ,, ,, 1776	such marks were rare.	19 ,, 1819 and so
Z ,, ,, 1777	From 1801 the following	on. After 1833 the date
	signs were used.	is given in full.

1 To recall the comet of 1769 some of the decorators substituted the mark ✳⤳ for the date-letter Q.

2 The insertion of the letters J and JJ in the Sèvres Guide (1909 edition), recently shown to have been used as date-letters, necessitated the alteration of the above tables to correspond.

MARK.	DESCRIPTION.	MARK.	DESCRIPTION.
	Sèvres		**Sèvres** Louis XVIII. 1814-24 the two last numbers of the year added from 1814. pr. in blue
	1792-1804 p. in blue and lilac		
	The First Republic		
	p. in blue		Charles X. 1824-28. pr. in blue
	1800-2 p. in gold and colours		
	1803 to May 8th 1804. Consular period		
			1829-30
	First Empire 1804-9. st. in red		1829-30
	1810-14. pr. in red		Louis-Philippe 1830

MARK.	DESCRIPTION.	MARK.	DESCRIPTION.
	Sèvres 1831-34 pr. in blue		**Sèvres** Second Republic 1848-52 pr. in red
	cypher of Louis Philippe		
			Second Empire 1852-4. pr. in red
	pr. in green		T = tendre, with reference to a soft paste made temporarily
	marks on wares destined for the Royal Châteaux. pr. in red		1854-70
			Third Republic 1880-89. pr. in red
	Also Château d'Eu 1846		1890-

MARK.	DESCRIPTION.	MARK.	DESCRIPTION.
(S. 71.)	1871 in red. The cut indicates a spoilt piece		Marks and monograms of painters, decorators, and gilders at Sèvres.
(S 1900)	1900 in green	$\mathcal{N}$	ALONCLE, birds, etc. 1758-81
		J.A.	ANDRÉ, Jules, landscapes, 1843-69
(A DORE SÈVRES R 1900 F)	1900-2 in red to indicate the gilding		ANTEAUME, landscapes, etc. 1754
		P.	APOIL, Alexis, figure subjects 1845-64
		EP.	APOIL, Mme., figures, 1864-1894
(RF DECORE A SÈVRES 1902)	1902-4 in red	$\mathcal{A}$	ARCHELAIS, decorator, 1865-1902
			ARMAND, birds, etc., 1745-1746
		A..A	ASSELIN, portraits, etc., 1750-94
(MINIST. DE L'AGR. ET DU COMM. RF)	1848 on porcelain made for Ministers pr. in red		AUBERT aîné, flowers, 1754-
		A	AUVILLAIN, ground colours 1877-
		P.A	AVISSE, decorator, 1850-1884
		By:	BAILLY fils, flowers, 1750-1800
(MINISTERE D'ETAT)		$\mathcal{B}$	BALLANGER, decorator, 1902
		.B	BARBIN, decorator, 1824-39
		=	BARDET, flowers, 1751-1800
(AMBASSADE DE FRANCE ST PETERSBOURG RF)	1898-1904 on porcelain made for various Embassies	83	BARRAT, bouquets, etc., 1780-91
		$\mathcal{O}3$	BARRE, detached bouquets, 1780-91
		AB	BARRÉ, flowers, 1846-81
(GARDE-MEUBLE DE L'ETAT)		$\mathcal{B}$	BARRIAT, figures, 1852-1883

Mark.	Description.	Mark.	Description.
6.D.	BAUDOIN, ornaments, 1750-	OB	BOULANGER, flowers, 1754-1800
Y	BECQUET, flowers, etc., 1748-	$	BOULANGER fils, subjects, 1770-81
B	BELET, E., flowers, etc., 1878-1900	Br	BRACHARD, sculptor
B	BELET, L., decorator, 1879-	By	BRÉCY, decorator, 1880-
B.r	BÉRANGER, figures, 1807-1846	Bn	BULIDON, bouquets, 1745-1792
G.	BERTRAND, bouquets, 1750-1800	MB	BUNEL, Mme., flowers, 1778-1817
B	BIEUVILLE, decorator, 1877-	⚓	BUTEUX père, flowers, 1756-1786
✶	BIENFAIT, gilding, 1756-	9.	BUTEUX fils aîné, flowers, 1773-1822
T.	BINET, bouquets, 1750-1800	△	BUTEUX fils jeune, subjects, 1780-94
Sc	BINET, Mme. (née Chanou), flowers, 1750-1800	Bx	BUTEUX, flowers, after 1800
B	BLANCHARD, decorator, 1811	X	CABAU, flowers, 1848-84
A.B	BLANCHARD, A., decorator, 1878-1900		
MB.	BOCQUET, decorator, 1902-	△	CAPELLE, borders, 1745-
B.T	BOITEL, gilding, 1797-1822	C.P	CAPRONNIER, gilding, 1800
AB	BONNUIT, decorator, 1858-1894	♀	CARDIN, bouquets, 1749-
🐦	BOUCHER, flowers, 1754-	5.	CARRIER, flowers, 1752-
🌳	BOUCHET, landscapes, etc., 1757-93	C.	CASTEL, landscapes, etc., 1750-1800
L.B.	BOUCOT, flowers, etc., 1785-91	Ch.C	CATTEAU, decorator, 1902-1904
Y.	BOUILLAT, flowers, etc., 1800-11	✳	CATON, subjects, etc., 1753
B	BOULLEMIER, gilding, 1822-1841	S	CATRICE, flowers, etc., before 1800
F.B	BOULLEMIER aîné, gilding, 1822-41	I.C	CÉLOS, decorator, 1865-1894
Bf	BOULLEMIER fils, gilding, 1802-12	ch.	CHABRY, subjects, etc., 1749

Mark.	Description.	Mark.	Description.
J.D.	CHANOU, Mme. (née Durosey), flowers, before 1800	C.D	DEVELLY, landscapes, etc., 1813-48
c.p	CHAPUIS ainé, flowers, etc., before, 1800	Đ	DEVICQ, decorator, 1880-
j.c.	CHAPUIS fils, bouquets, before 1800	D.h	DEUTSCH, decorator, 1805-1817
L.C.	CHARPENTIER, decorator, after 1800	D.Í.	DIDIER, decorator, 1819-1845
F.C	CHARRIN, Mme., subjects, etc., after 1800	△	DIEU, Chinese subjects gilding, before 1800
✹	CHAVAUX père, gilding, 1752-	Đ	DOAT, sculptor, 1878-
j.n	CHAVAUX fils, gilding, etc., 1770-83	K	DODIN, figures, etc., 1754-1803
♦	CHEVALLIER, flowers, 1755	D.R	DRAUD, Chinese figures and gilding, before 1800
★	CHOISY, de, flowers, etc., 1800-1817	Đ	DROUET, decorator, 1879-
ℰ	CHULOT, flowers, etc., 1755	D.T.	DROUET, flowers, 1828
C.M.	COMMELIN, bouquets, before 1800	✳	DUBOIS, flowers, etc., 1756-
·C.C.	CONSTANT, gilding, 1804-1815	A.D.	DUCLUZEAU, Mme., figures, etc., 1818-48
C.T.	CONSTANTIN, figures, 1823-1845	D.y	DUROSEY, gilding, 1802-27
♪	CORNAILLE, flowers, 1755-1793	D.	DUSOLLE, bouquets, before 1800
ℛC.	COURCY, de, figures, 1866-1886	D T	DUTANDA, bouquets, before 1800
L.	COUTURIER, gilding, 1783-	LD	EAUBONNE, d', decorator, 1904
A	COURSAJET, decorator, †1886	Æ	ESCALLIER, Mme., decorator, 1874-88
A	DAMMOUSE, figures, etc., 1862-80	⚹	EVANS, birds, insects, etc., 1752-
Đ	DAVID, decorator, 1852-1882	F	FALOT, birds, insects, etc., before 1800
D.F.	DAVIGNON, landscapes, 1814	HF	FARAGUET, Mme., figures, 1856-70
D.F.	DELAFOSSE, figures, 1805-1815	ℱ	FICQUENET, flowers, 1864-1881
D.P.	DESPERAIS, decorator, 1794-1822	❧	FONTAINE, miniatures, etc., 1752
DG	DERICHSWEILER, G., decorator, 1858-84		

Mark.	Description.	Mark.	Description.
F	FONTAINE, flowers, 1827-1857		GOMERY, flowers, 1756
♡	FONTELLIAU, gilding, 1753-	*F.G*	GOUPIL, figures, 1863-79
Y	FOURÉ, flowers, before 1800	*G t.*	GRÉMONT, bouquets, 1770-1781
Æ	FOURNERIE, decorator, 1903	*X*	GRISON, gilding, 1749
A.F	FOURNIER, decorator, 1878-	*G*	GUILLEMAIN, decorator, after 1800
UhB	FRAGONARD, figures, etc., 1847-69	*H*	HALLION, E., landscapes, 1884
☀	FRITSCH, figures, etc., 1763-1765	*H.*	HALLION, Fr., gilder, 1866-1895
E.F	FROMENT, figures	*jh.*	HENRION, bouquets, before 1784
ft.fx	FUMEZ, bouquets, 1777-1801	*hc.*	HÉRICOURT, bouquets before 1800
Gu.	GANEAU fils, gilding, after 1800	*W.*	HILKEN, figures, etc., before 1800
❀	GAUTHIER, landscapes, etc., 1787-91	*H*	HOURY, flowers, 1747-55
Œ	GÉBLEUX, decorator, 1883-	*h.ɔ.*	HUARD, decorator, 1811-1846
J.G.	GÉLY, decorator, 1851-1888	*E.h.*	HUMBERT, figures, 1862-1870
G	GENEST, figures, 1752	*hy*	HUNY, flowers, 1791-99
†	GENIN, flowers, etc., 1756	*Ė*	JARDEL, decorator, 1836-
G.G.	GEORGET, figures, etc., 1802-23	*Z*	JOYAU, bouquets, before 1800
Gd.	GÉRARD, subjects, before 1800	*j.*	JUBIN, gilding, before 1800
γ.t	GÉRARD, Mme. (née Vautrin), flowers, before 1800	*Ė*	JULIENNE, renaissance ornaments, after 1800
R	GIRARD, Chinese figures, before 1800	*H*	LAMBERT, flowers, 1864-96
Gob.R	GOBERT, figures, 1852-91	*LGo*	LANGLACÉ, landscapes, 1813-44
Jx	GOBLED, decorator, 1902-	*h.LR*	LA ROCHE, flowers, before 1800
D.G.	GODIN, gilding, 1808-28	*H*	LASSERRE, decorator, 1896-

Mark.	Description.	Mark.	Description.
ℐℒ	LATACHE, gilding, after 1800	ℳℰ	MAUGENDRE, sculptor, 1881-86
ℒ͞	LE BEL aîné, figures, etc., before 1800	Éde M	MAUSSION, Mme. de, figures 1860-70
ℒℬ.	LE BEL jeune, bouquets, 1780-93	ſ	MÉRAULT aîné, decorator, 1754-91
ℒ.ℬ.	LE BEL, landscapes, 1804-1844	9	MÉRAULT jeune, bouquets, 1786-89
✲	LÉANDRE, subjects, left in 1785	ℳ	MÉRIGOT, decorator, 1848-1884
L	LECAT, ground colours, 1872-	ℳℛ	MEYER, A., figures, 1863-1871
ℒℒ LL	LECOT, Chinese subjects, before 1800	X	MICAUD, flowers, 1759
◡	LEDOUX, landscapes, etc., 1758	.ℳ C	MICAUD, gilding, 1792-1812
A	LÉGER, decorator, 1902-	Mou M	MICHEL, bouquets, before 1800
ℒℊ.ℒℊ	LE GUAY, gilding, 1748	ℳ	MILET, O., decorator, 1862-1877
ℒ.ℊ.	LE GUAY, figures, etc., 1778-81	L M	MIMARD, decorator, 1884-
ℒ.	LE GAY, decorator, 1866-1884	M	MOIRON, bouquets, 1790-1791
◊	LEGUAY, miniatures, etc., 1772-1817	5.	MOUGENOT, flowers, 1754
ℒℊ	LEGRAND, gilding, after 1800	ℳℛ	MOREAU, gilding, 1809-15
EL.	LEROY, gilding, 1864-88	ℳ	MORIN, naval and military subjects, 1754
ℒou L	LEVÉ père, flowers, etc., 1754	ℳ	MORIN, gilding, 1888-
ƒ	LEVÉ, F., flowers, etc., before 1800	AM	MORIOT, figures, 1830-48
AL	LIGNÉ, decorator, 1883-	ʌ	MUTEL, landscapes, 1754
CL	LUCAS, decorator, 1878-	n q	N.QUET, bouquets, left in 1792
ℛℬ	MAQUERET, Mme. (née Bouillat), flowers, before 1800	⌒	NOËL, flowers, etc., 1755
⌀	MARTINET, flowers, 1861-1878	ℐD	NOUAILHIER, Mme. (née Durosey), flowers, before 1800
ℳ	MASSY, flowers, 1779-1806	o.ch	OUINT, Ch., decorator, 1879-82

Mark.	Description.	Mark.	Description.
E	OUINT, E., coloured grounds, 1888-93		QUENNOY, decorator, 1902
Q	OUINT, Em., coloured grounds, 1877-89		RAUX, bouquets, before 1800
P	PAILLET, figures, 1882-88	*R*	RÉGNIER, F., figures, 1820-1866
P	PARPETTE, flowers, etc., 1755	*JR*	RÉGNIER, H., figures, 1825-1870
P.P.	PARPETTE, Mme., flowers, etc., 1794	*R*	RÉJOUX, gilding, 1862-90
L.P.	PARPETTI, Mme., L., flowers, 1789-1825		RENARD, E., decorator, after 1800
	PAJOU, sculptor, 1750	*H.R.*	RENARD, H., decorator, 1881
P	PELUCHE, decorator, 1880-	*MR*	RICHARD, Em., flowers, 1869-1900
P.T.	PETIT, flowers, 1756	ER	RICHARD, E., flowers, 1838-1872
f	PFEIFFER, bouquets, before 1800		RICHARD, F., decorator, 1848-78
P.H.	PHILIPPINE aîné, subjects 1780-91	*Jh.R*	RICHARD, S., decorator, 1832
P.h.	PHILIPPINE, flowers, 1787-1791	LR	RICHARD, L., decorator, 1902
pᵛ	PIERRE aîné, flowers, before 1800	✳	RICHARD, P., gilding, 1849-1881
p.j.	PIERRE jeune, bouquets, before 1800	*Rx.*	RIOCREUX, I., landscapes, 1824-49
P	PIHAN, decorator, 1888-	*Rx*	RIOCREUX, D., flowers, 1807-72
P.t.	PITHOU aîné, subjects, before 1800	PR	ROBERT, P., landscapes, 1806-43
P.j.	PITHOU jeune, figures, etc., before 1800	CR	ROBERT, Mme., flowers, after 1800
P	PLINE, gilding, 1831	*R*	ROBERT, J. F., landscapes, 1806-12
P	PORCHON, gilding	XX	ROCHER, figures, etc., 1758
Q	POUILLOT, bouquets, before 1778		ROSSET, landscapes, 1753
A	POUPART, landscapes, 1815-45	*R.L.*	ROUSSEL, bouquets, before 1800
HP.	PREVOST, gilding, 1754	PMR	ROUSSEL, figures, 1842-72

Mark.	Description.	Mark.	Description.
	SANDOZ, decorator, 1890-		TROYON, decorator, 1802-1817
P.S.	SCHILT, L., flowers, 1822-55		ULRICH, decorator, 1889-1904
S.h.	SCHADRE, birds, etc., before 1800		VANDÉ, gilding, etc., 1753
	SIEFFERT, figures, 1883-88	W	VAVASSEUR, arabesques, 1753
E.S	SIMARD, decorator, 1883-		VIEILLARD, decorator, 1752-90
	SINSSON, flowers, 1780-95		VIGNOL, decorator, 1883-
S.S.p	SINSSON, flowers, 1820-25	2000	VINCENT, gilding, 1752-91
	SIOUX aîné, bouquets, 1752-1792	W	WALTER, flowers, 1832-82
O	SIOUX jeune, flowers, 1752-1792		WEYDINGER, gilding, c. 1814
	SOLON, M., figures, etc., 1862-71		XROWET, flowers, etc., 1750
S.W.	SWEBACH, landscapes, 1806-1814		YVERNEL, landscapes, etc., 1750
	TABARY, birds, 1754		**Decorators who signed in full**
	TAILLANDIER, bouquets, 1753-90		ANDRÉ, J., landscapes, 1843-1869
• • •	TANDART, flowers, 1755		BALDISSERONI, figures, 1865-1879
	TARDI, bouquets, 1757-95		BARRIAT, decorator, 1852-1883
• • • •	THÉODORE, gilding, before 1800		BÉRANGER, J., figures, 1807-1846
	THÉVENET père, flowers, etc., 1745		BOIS, Th. du., sea subjects, 1842-1848
jt.	THÉVENET fils, decorator, 1752		BOQUET, landscapes, 1804-1814
J.T.	TRAGER, J., flowers, etc. 1841-73		BOQUET (Mlle. Virginie), landscapes, 1835-1863
H	TRAGER, H., decorator, 1887-		BUCQ (Le), landscapes, 1843 BULOT, flowers, 1862-1883 BRUNEL, figures, 1863-1883
.I	TRAGER, L., decorator, 1888-		CABAU, C., flowers, 1848-1884
	TRISTAN, decorator, 1879-1882		CÉLOS, J., decorator, 1865-1894 COOL (Mme. de), figures, 1870 COURCY (de), figures, 1866-1884

DEGAULT, figures, 1808-1817
DEMARNE, subjects, 1808-1814
DEMARNE (Mlle. Caroline), landscapes, 1822-1825
DENOIS (Mlle. Jenny), portraits, 1820
DESBOIS, sculptor, 1886-1887
DEVELLY, C., landscapes, 1813-1848
DIDIER, decorator, 1819-1845
DUCLUZEAU (Mme. Adelaïde), portraits, 1809-1848
DUFRESNE, Henry, figures, 1862
FONTAINE, flowers, etc., 1850
FRAGONARD, Th., subjects, 1847-1869
FROMENT DELORMEL, Eug., figures, 1853-1884
GALLOIS (Mme.), figures, 1871
GARNERAY, L., sea subjects, 1838-1842
GÉLY, J., figures, 1851-1888
GEORGET, figures, 1803-1806
GODDÉ, enamels and reliefs, 1861-1863
HAMON, figures, 1849-1854
JACCOBER, flowers and fruit, 1818-1848
JADELOT (Mme. S.), subjects, 1864-1871
JAQUOTOT (Mme. Victoire), portraits, 1801-1842
LABBÉ, flowers, 1847-1853
LAMARRE, landscapes
LAMBERT, landscapes, 1858
LASSERRE, decorator, 1896-
LAURENT (Mme. Pauline), figures, etc., 1850

LANGLACÉ, landscapes, 1807-1844
LANGLOIS (Polyclès), landscapes, 1847-1872
LEBEL, portraits, etc., 1804-1844
LEGUAY, subjects, figures, 1778-1840
LESSORRE, figures, 1834
LYNYBYE, landscapes, 1841-1842
MERIGOT, F., flowers, etc., 1848-1888
MEYER-HEINE, figures, 1862-1868
MORIOT, figures, portraits, 1830-1848
PARENT, L.-B., figures, 1816
PHILIP, enamels, 1847-1877
PHILIPPINE, still life, 1785-1840
POUPART, A., landscapes, 1815-1845
RÉGNIER, landscapes, 1836-1870
RICHARD, E., decorator, 1858
ROBERT, landscapes, 1806-1843
RODIN, sculptor, 1881-1883
ROUSSEL (P.-M.), figures, 1848-1872
SCHILT (L.-P.), flowers, 1822-1855
SCHILT (Abel), figures, 1847-1880
SOLON (Mlle. L.), figures, 1862-1871
SWEBACH, landscapes, etc., 1806-1814
TRAGER, J., birds, etc., 1841-187?
TREVERRET (de), figures, 1819
TRISTAN, figures, 1863
TURGAN (Mme. Constance), portraits, 1834
VAN OS, flowers and fruits, 1811-1814
VAN MARCK, subjects, 1825-1862
VERDIER, J., designer, vers, 1890

SPAIN AND PORTUGAL

THE manufactory of a tin-enamelled earthenware decorated in blue, manganese and green, or in blue and lustre pigment, or in lustre alone, flourished in Spain from an early date, and was most probably introduced by the Moors.   Manises and Valencia were centres of the industry, which was at its best in the fifteenth and sixteenth centuries.   In the seventeenth century several Italian potters settled in Spain, and introduced the manufacture of their, then decadent, maiolica there.   Later, when French faïence was at its height, some French potters removed to Spain, so that during the seventeenth and eighteenth centuries tin-enamelled wares were made at Alcora, Talavera, and elsewhere, some of which recall the later styles of Italian maiolica, while others resemble French faïence.   Wall-tiles with elaborate geometrical patterns of Moorish origin, known as *azulejos,* were largely made in Spain from early times, and formed a special industry.

Porcelain was manufactured in due course in the eighteenth century, the most important factory being that of Buen Retiro, near Madrid, founded in 1760 by the help of workmen and moulds removed from Capo-di-Monte, Naples.   The ware was at first a soft paste, but after 1780 a harder magnesian porcelain was made.

Clever copies of Palissy ware and the mottled earthenwares of Staffordshire are made by Mafra, at Caldas, in Portugal.

MARK.	DESCRIPTION.	MARK.	DESCRIPTION.
	Hispano-Moresque pottery 15th cent. **Valencia**	A AL CO᷉ ᴀ2 CRᵒS P.c	**Alcora** Pottery and porcelain 18th cent.
		ALCORA ESPÂNA Soliva FABRICA REAL DE ALCORA ANO 1735 CHRIS·OVALE:OS	Painters' initials A = Albaro E = Escuder M = Mas
	15th cent.		
	c. 1480	MOX Fo Fev VCᵒ J Albarez f·	Painters' marks
	? Manises 1610 (and a hand in a circle)		**Talavera** 17th and 18th cent.
	Puente de Arzobispo 16th and 17th cent.	S ⛤ L ᴀᴠ	**Seville** 19th cent.
	Alcora 18th cent. "A" mark after 1784	*De la Real Fabrica de Azulejos de Valencia* *Soc de Juana Zamore* *Real Fabrica de Dᵒ Maria Salvador*	1836 ? Valencia, 1786 **Disdier** 1808

MARK.	DESCRIPTION.	MARK.	DESCRIPTION.
P.Y.C 12	Seville Early 19th cent.	UIANNA V V	Viana de Castello 18th cent.
PICKMAN Y.CA. CHINAOPACA SEVILLA		Rossi 1785	Coimbra
VEGA	Valladolid ? 18th cent.	MAFRA CALDAS	Caldas c. 1870 Imitations of Palissy ware
REAL FABRICA SARGADELOS	Sargadelos 19th cent.	IAG	Lisbon c. 1833
SEGOVIA	Segovia 19th cent.		Buen Retiro (Madrid) 1760-1804. Soft paste till about 1780, and afterwards a hard hybrid porcelain p. in blue and imp.
R R	Portugal Porto Pottery of Massarellos 1738-1833	F.C.	
M.P. MIRAGAIA	Miragaïa c. 1755	F Z	
F, R,	Rato 18th cent.		

MARK.	DESCRIPTION.	MARK.	DESCRIPTION.
Giuseppe Fumo	**Buen Retiro** Porcelain	J 22 ↑	**Buen Retiro** 1804-8
Carl✱ Gr		S R	
G G 7		V M	
JOSEPH GRICC¹	c. 1763	Velazg²	
✱ F o-	c. 1803	NA JL HAGRAN DE J.M PEREIRA	**Portugal** **Lisbon** J. Ferreira 19th cent.
S N 1775		LISBOA 1793	Lisbon
N. D.		VA	**Vista Alegre** 1790-
HC		V.A. △	
R F E PORCELANA E S M C			
J ♔G M^D S P S	1804-8		**Malta** c. 1844 Stoneware
R MADRID S			

THE BRITISH ISLES

VARIOUS attempts to make porcelain in the neighbourhood of London culminated in factories at Bow and Chelsea, both of which were active as early as 1745. The ware was a soft-paste porcelain, the secret of which had been learnt, no doubt, from French potters. Shortly after 1750 other factories sprung up at Derby, Worcester, Lowestoft, Longton Hall, Bristol, and Liverpool. All the early English porcelains were varieties of soft-paste, some distinguished by the admixture of bone-ash, and others by that of steatite. The only true hard-paste porcelain was made of Cornish materials at Plymouth from 1768-70 and at Bristol from 1770-81. The English porcelains continued to vary under fresh experiments till the end of the eighteenth century, when a more permanent mixture was arrived at by Josiah Spode in Staffordshire. This was the modern English porcelain, made chiefly of China clay and China stone from Cornwall, and bone-ash; it combines the strength of hard-paste with some of the soft mellowness of the old soft-paste porcelain. The decoration passed through regular phases, first copying the Chinese white wares, then the blue and white, then the enamelled Japanese porcelain exported from Imari; next came imitations of the Meissen and Sèvres styles, from the rococo to the pseudo-classical; and at the beginning of the nineteenth century the Japan patterns were revived in a very free rendering of the more elaborate "Imari" designs. After this the potters fell back on imitations of the earlier styles until new life was infused into their work at the end of the last century.

Marked specimens of English earthenware are practically unknown before the seventeenth century. It was then that delft or tin-enamelled ware in the Dutch fashion began to be made, chiefly at Lambeth: this industry spread over the country in the eighteenth century, and considerable factories sprung up at Bristol and Liverpool. In Staffordshire and at Wrotham in Kent, in Derbyshire and other places the more English method of decorating earthenware with coloured slips was largely practised, and many of the pieces bear the names or initials of potters as well as those of the destined possessors of the pots. At the end of the seventeenth century salt-glazed stoneware was made by Dwight of Fulham, and at Nottingham, and a fine red stoneware after the Chinese *buccaro* was made by Dwight and by Elers in Staffordshire. Early in the eighteenth century the Staffordshire potters became celebrated for a fine, white, salt-glazed stoneware of remarkable thinness and sharpness which is called "salt-glaze" par excellence. This was followed by a lead-glazed earthenware of creamy-yellow tone perfected by Wedgwood in his Queen's ware about 1760. It was decorated, first with splashes and mottlings of green and brown or brownish-purples, and afterwards by painting in enamel colours. Towards the end of the century numerous earthenwares and stonewares were invented or perfected by Josiah Wedgwood and his contemporaries, *e.g.* jasper wares, black basalt or Egyptian black, cane-coloured stoneware, pearl-ware, etc. ; and in the early nineteenth century a host of iron-stone chinas, improved stone chinas, etc., mostly hard white earthen-wares, were invented as cheap substitutes for porcelain. Marks on English pottery are mostly impressed and are often difficult to decipher because the glaze has filled up the hollows of the stamp.

MARK.	DESCRIPTION.	MARK.	DESCRIPTION.
	? John Bacon on Bow porcelain inc.		? Bow or Chelsea c. 1750 p. in blue
	Belleek Co. Fermanagh Ireland 1857- Pr.		**Bristol** 1770-81 h.p. The Meissen cross swords borrowed by Champion. p. in blue. The numbers 1-17 probably indicate different painters. Bone and Stephens are said to have been 1 and 2
	Bow 1745-76 s. p. inc.		
	p. in red		
	p. in blue		Plymouth and Bristol marks combined
			A leaf painted over the word 'Bristoll' in raised letters
			Tebo, modeller (see above) inc.
	This and the trident-shaped mark above also occur on Worcester Porcelain		In low reliefs. Mark of an early factory, c. 1750
	Tebo modeller inc.	Bristoll	**Caughley** 1772-1814 s. p. p. in blue These works were absorbed by Coalport. S = Salopian.
	? Bow		Disguised numeral resembling an Oriental mark

MARK.	DESCRIPTION.	MARK.	DESCRIPTION.
	Caughley 1772-1814 s.p. p. in blue	*Chelsea*	**Chelsea** c. 1745-84 s.p. Period I. c. 1745-50 triangle mark inc.
			Period II. 1750-c. 1753. Anchor in relief on an oval pad
			Same mark out- lined in red
	? Caughley		Anchor in blue
SALOPIAN	Caughley and **Coalport** 1780 onwards CBD = Colebrookdale		Period III. c. 1753-8. Anchor in red
			Period IV. 1759-70. Anchor in gold
		R	Roubiliac, sculptor. inc.
	Monogram of C. S. with letters C = Caughley, S = Swansea, N = Nantgarw, factories absorbed by Coalport; used since c. 1860		Early mark copy- ing a Chinese seal p. in red
JOHN ROSE & CO. COLEBROOK DALE 1850			Period V. 1770-84
ENGLAND **COALPORT** A.D. 1750	Modern mark pr.		Chelsea-Derby period, during which Duesbury of Derby owned the works
	Imitation of Sèvres on blue printed ware		p. in gold and colours
Coalport.			

MARK.	DESCRIPTION.	MARK.	DESCRIPTION.
DONOVAN 481 Donovan's Irish Manufacture	Donovan of Poolbeg St., Dublin, decorated Minton and other porcelains c. 1800 p. in red		**Derby** pr. in red c. 1830-48
	Derby s. p. p. blue 1770-84	BLOOR. DERBY.	pr. in red
125	Crown Derby mark painted in colours c. 1782 onwards. Early marks in blue, puce, or gold, later in red	D	pr. in red
D		D	on imitations of Sèvres
N 384 N° 3 6 3	Incised on figures and vases, pattern numbers and workmen's marks added: *e.g.* triangle for Hill; star for Farnsworth	X · · X	Derby porcelain with Meissen mark
		DERBY·	Rare mark in blue, on porcelain printed by Holdship at Derby c. 1764
N	inc.		Copy of Chinese tripod mark
Wo 10	inc.	G Cocker ·O	Cocker, figure maker at Derby early 19th cent. and in London c. 1840- inc.
2 Size G		LOCKER & Cº LATE BLOOR DERBY	King Street c. 1850 after the closing of the old factory pr.
BK	Monogram of Duesbury and Kean, 1795-7 p. in colour		

Mark.	Description.	Mark.	Description.
	Derby King St. c. 1870 Initials of Stevenson and S. Hancock pr. in red	☽ w	**Lowestoft** copies of Worcester marks.
	Mark of the Royal Crown Derby Factory in Osmaston Rd. 1876- pr.	*J. Sadler, Liverpool* *Sadler, Lip*[l] *Sadler, Lip*[l]*, enam*[l] *Evans, sculpsit* *Gilbody, maker*	**Liverpool** Sadler and Green printers, 1756-99 (see p. 103) c. 1770
Shore & Co	**Isleworth** Shore & Goulding 1760-c. 1800 s.p. p. in colour	HERCULANEUM	Herculaneum works c. 1800-41 (see p. 103)
Allen *Lowestoft*	**Lowestoft** 1757-1802 s.p. Allen, painter late 18th cent.	NANT-GARW C.W. G	**Nantgarw** China works. Co. Glamorgan 1813-14 and 1817-20 s.p. mark imp.
J V IV VI 3 5 16 ♀	Numbers (7 to 25) and workmen's mark on Lowestoft porcelain. p. in blue	N P P B 26	**Pinxton** (Derbyshire) s.p. 1796-1812. p. in colour ? initial of Billingsley
ℋ ℱ x N ℒ A 4[E] G 11 D mi.	Imitation Chinese marks. p. blue	*Billingsley* *Mansfield* 2|4 2|4 24	Billingsley decorated various wares at Mansfield in 1801 **Plymouth** h.p. 1768-70. works removed to Bristol in 1770 and converted into the Bristol China manufactory in 1773. p. in blue and colours

MARK.	DESCRIPTION.	MARK.	DESCRIPTION.
griffin crest *Rockingham Works Brameld* BRAMELD	**Rockingham** Porcelain made by Brameld 1820-42 pr. in a wreath	COPELAND COPELAND&GARRETT LATE SPODE COPELAND	**Staffordshire** *Stoke-upon-Trent* W. Copeland bought Spode's business in 1833 Garrett a partner 1835-47 pr.
X DL J F N	**Staffordshire** *Longton Hall* Littler & Co. 1752-58 s.p. p. in blue *New Hall* c. 1781-1825 s.p.	M. B. MINTON & BOYLE M. & Co. MINTON MINTONS	Minton 1796 onwards p. in colour The ermine mark after 1851. Minton and Boyle 1836-42 imp. since 1861 imp. Modern mark pr.
(New Hall)	pr. in red	DAVENPORT DAVENPORT LONGPORT	*Longport* Davenport 1794-1887 pr. in red
ſpode SPODE Spode felspar Porcelain SPODE COPELAND	**Stoke-upon-Trent** Spode 1797-1833 p. in colours and gold in a wreath pr. Copeland was Spode's London agent and afterwards partner	 *Warburtons Patent 667* *Lane End, july* 1787 TURNER *Turner's Patent*	P. Warburton *New Hall* patent for printing in gold, 1810 W. & J. Turner of *Lane End* with or without Prince of Wales' feathers. Patent for improvements in porcelain, 1809

MARK.	DESCRIPTION.	MARK.	DESCRIPTION.
MILES MASON M. MASON	**Staffordshire** M. Mason at *Lane Delph* c. 1804 pr. imp.	*Decorated by* SWANSEA *H. Morris*	**Swansea** Morris continued to paint porcelain of various kinds at Swansea after 1824
Shorthose & Cº CC	*Hanley* c. 1820 p. in blue	*Pardoe, Bristol*	1809-20 (cf. p. 104)
RILEY 1823	*Burslem* 1814-26 imp.		**Worcester** 1751 onwards s.p. crescent used alone from c. 1751-1793 p. and pr. in blue
WEDGWOOD	Stencilled in red or blue, 1805-15 (cf. p. 113)		on painted and blue printed wares
R W. T. ENGLISH PORCELAIN J. R. & Co.	Occurs on porcelain made by Hilditch (see p. 111) and others Ridgway 1814-55 pr.		c. 1751-1783. Imitations of Oriental marks. p. in blue
IBS	Early 19th cent.		
Swansea	**Swansea** 1814-24 s.p. p. in red		Copy of the Chinese jade mark
SWANSEA	1815-17 imp.		Copies of Meissen, Chelsea, Sèvres, and Tournay marks
SWANSEA	Also the name SWANSEA stencilled		

MARK.	DESCRIPTION.	MARK.	DESCRIPTION.
	Worcester s.p. Workmen's marks 1751-83 Similar marks occur on Lowestoft and Bow porcelains. p. in blue	*Chamberlains Worcester* CHAMBERLAIN 	**Worcester** Chamberlain's factory, 1789-1840 With other marks giving the address of the London house pr.
	Flight period 1783-93. The mark FLIGHTS incised occurs rarely. B incised for Barr (1793-1803). Flight & Barr 1793-1807 Barr, Flight, and Barr, 1807-13	*George Grainger Royal China Works Worcester* *Grainger Lee & Co Worcester*	Grainger's factory 1801-1888
	Flight, Barr, and Barr, 1813-40 1851-62. This mark under a crown 1862 onwards. pr.		pr.
	Marks of R. Hancock (1756-74), engraver. The anchor for ? R. Holdship On printed ware Painter of animals. (Monogram of JD for John Donaldson, also occurs on vases, c. 1768)	 	1896-1905 pr. pr.

MARK.	DESCRIPTION.	MARK.	DESCRIPTION.
Absolon Yarmᵗ	**Yarmouth** a decorator late 18th cent.	MALING FRUIT BASKET W. S. & Co.	**North Hylton** 1762—moved to Newcastle in 1817
Belle Vue Pottery *Hull.*	**Hull** 1826-41 pr.		**Stockton-on-Tees** W. Smith & Co. 1820- pr.
DAWSON & CO. O	**Hylton** 1800- imp.		
FERRYBRIDGE.	**Ferrybridge** 1792-early 19th cent.		
F. WEDGWOOD.		W. S. & Co. QUEENS WARE STOCKTON	
WEDGWOOD & CO.	1796-	W. S. & Co. WEDGEWOOD	also S. & W.
Tomlinson & Co.	1792-96 and 1801-34		
FELL, NEWCASTLE	**Newcastle** 1817-	SEWELLS & DONKIN	**Newcastle** St. Antony's. c. 1780-
F ⚓		DIXON, AUSTIN & CO. SUNDERLAND	**Sunderland** 1800-
MIDDLESBRO POTTERY CO	**Middlesboro** 1831-44 imp.	I. W. & Co.	
LONDON ⚓	,,	PHILLIPS & CO.	
J. PHILLIPS HYLTON POTTERY	1817- See above	ROCKINGHAM	**Rockingham** 1765-1843 (cf. p. 99)
SCOTT *Brothers & Co.*	**Southwick** 1789-	BRAMELD	(the same in a wreath)
Moore & Co. Stoneware Southwick	Wear Pottery 1803-	MORTLOCK'S CADOGAN	Early 19th cent.
		DON POTTERY	**Swinton** 1790 onwards

Mark.	Description.	Mark.	Description.
  D. D. & Co. CASTLEFORD	**Swinton** Don Pottery 1790 onwards **Castleford** late 18th cent. onwards. David Dunderdale & Co. (1803-21)	**P** $\flat$	**Liverpool** Pennington 18th cent. p. in blue
  HARTLEY, GREENS & CO. LEEDS * POTTERY	interlaced Ds ? David Dunderdale **Leeds** c. 1760-1878 imp.	*J. Sadler, Liverp*[l] *Sadler, sculp*[t] *Green, Liverpl.* *J. Johnson* HERCULANEUM POTTERY	Sadler and Green, printers and potters 1756-99. Sadler retired about 1774 Engraver c. 1790 Herculaneum pottery 1794-1841
			pr. ,,
L. P. R. B. & S. *Nottn.* 1703 *Made at Nottingham ye 17th day of August* A.D. 1771	Leeds Pottery R. Britton and Sons 1863-78 L for Leeds (in a quatrefoil within a circle) **Nottingham** stoneware	 pr. ,,
		 CAMBRIDGE	pattern mark on Liverpool ware pr.
		BELPER & DENBY BOURNE'S POTTERIES DERBYSHIRE J. BOURNE & SON BOURNE'S POTTERIES DENBY & CODNOR PARK DERBYSHIRE	**Belper** 1800-34. **Denby** 1812 onwards **Codnor Park** Pottery taken by Bourne in 1833 and closed 1861

MARK.	DESCRIPTION.	MARK.	DESCRIPTION.
J. OLDFIELD & CO.	**Chesterfield**	*J. Eaves, Bristol*	**Bristol** on earthenware early 19th cent.
S. M. 1726	**Derby** slip ware. ? Samuel Meir	*J. Doe*, 1797	painter
R S		W. F., 1848	W. Fifield, painter (b. 1777, d. 1857)
John Meir, 1708		POUNTNEY & ALLIES	1816-35
S S *By Stephen Shaw* 1725	incised	POWELL, BRISTOL	Mid. 19th cent.
I H	John Heath c. 1770 cream ware	*Marthar Wilkinson Bristol Pottery*, 1808	painter : mark incised
Pot Works in Derby	pr. c. 1770	*Pardoe, fecit, Bristol*	1809-20
Radford Sculpsit		*Crickmay Potter, Weymouth*	**Weymouth** c. 1840 imp.
	Lowesby c. 1835 imp.	WINCANTO *Nathaniel Ireson*, 1748	**Wincanton** delft ware c. 1730-50
	Bristol delft ware 18th cent.	P. P. Coy. L. *Stone, China*	**Plymouth** Pottery Co. c. 1850
	? Flower	T. M. 1790	**Donyat** (Somerset) graffiato ware
1761 Bowen fecit	p. in blue	J. G. Mkr. 1669	**Welsh** graffiato ware
	cream ware 1786-c. 1840	*James Daves Pencoyd*	**Pencoyd** Glamorganshire 1822
+	? Bristol	*Cambrian Pottery*	**Swansea** earthenware 1769-1870

MARK.	DESCRIPTION.	MARK.	DESCRIPTION.
CAMBRIAN	**Swansea** Cambrian Works 1769-1870.	RICHARD NORMAN	**Chailey** (near Rye) 1842
		I. L. 1638	**Wrotham** (Kent) slip ware probably initials of the potters
SWANSEA		G. R. 1651	
DILLWYN & CO.	1813-50	I. W. 1656	
Swansea		H. I. 1669	? Jull
DILLWYN'S ETRUSCAN WARE	1848-9	N. H. 1678	
		I. E. 1697	
BEVINGTON & CO.	1817-24	IE WE 1699 WROTHAM	
		Kishere, Mortlake	**Mortlake** early 19th cent.
CUBA DILLWYN & Cº	pr.	SOUTH WALES POTTERY S. W. P.	**Llanelly** 1839——
Opaque China B. B. & I.	Glamorgan Works Baker, Bevans and Irwin 1816-39	*Fulham Pottery*	**Fulham** early 19th cent. mark
OPAQUE CHINA B. B. & I. 4	pr.	*T. Wetherill Modeler No.* 1 *Cleaver St., Lambeth, London*	**Lambeth** stoneware 19th cent.
Rye (*Sussex*) *Pottery*	**Rye** c. 1790 onwards Cadborough Works	*Stephen Green Lambeth*	c. 1837 imp.
R S X W RYE	Bellevue Works 1869 onwards		

MARK.	DESCRIPTION.	MARK.	DESCRIPTION.
Doulton & Watts Lambeth Pottery	**Lambeth** 1820-58 stoneware	CARTWRIGHT	**Staffordshire** c. 1650
		JOSEPH GLASS	1703
J. & M. P. B. & Co.	**Glasgow** Bell and Co. 1842-	*Thomas Heath, 1677*	? Derby
		Job Heath, 1702	,,
SCOTT PB 6	**Portobello** late 18th cent. onwards	*Joshua Heath, 1771*	,,
		Richard Meir	c. 1708
		John Meir, 1708	
	Dublin ? delft ware c. 1770	*Richard Mare, 1696*	
		Richard Meer, 1680	
		W. RICH, 1702	
Dublin		TH. SANS, 1650	? Wrotham
WOODNORTH & CO.	? Staffordshire 1818	R. SHAW, 1692	
		JOHN SIMPSON, 1735	
Engraved by James Brindley	Staffordshire	RALPH SIMPSON	c. 1700
		WILLIAM SIMPSON	1685
Belfast 1724 M H·R 1724	**Belfast** on delft ware	THOMAS TOFT, 1671	
		RALPH TOFT, 1676	
	Fremington (N. Devon) Fishley's factory c. 1860	JAMES TOFT, 1705	
John Pidler his hand		CHARLES TOFT	Modern
John Hoyle	**Bideford** c. 1860	RALPH TURNOR, 1680 WILLIAM TALOR GEORGE TAYLOR, 1690	
John Phillip Hoyle	1852 graffiato and slip wares	JOHN TAYLOR, 1700 JOHN WRIGHT, 1707 JOHN WEDGWOOD 1691	All in this column are makers of slip-ware

MARK.	DESCRIPTION.	MARK.	DESCRIPTION.
	Staffordshire		**Stoke-upon-Trent**
	On red stoneware made by Elers at Bradwell (1690-1710) and afterwards by many 18th cent. potters imp.	M. & C.	1793 onwards Minton and Co.
		B. B. *New Stone*	
		M. &. B.	Minton and Boyle
		MINTON	See p. 99
	On a black teapot supposed to have been made by Twyford early 18th cent.		c. 1824 pr.
		R. WOOD	**Burslem**
		36 Ra Wood Burslem	Ralph Wood b. 1716, d. 1772 and his son of same name b. 1748, d. 1797. b. 1759-d. 1840
	? Twyford's mark inc.	ENOCH WOOD	
		ENOCH WOOD & CO.	
		WOOD & CALDWELL BURSLEM	1790-1818
			1818-46
	Saltglaze		
	marks on saltglaze are very rare	LAKIN	1770-1795
		LAKIN & POOLE	,,
W. T. & Co.	? William Taylor & Co. c. 1760	R. POOLE	1795-
SPODE C	**Stoke-upon-Trent**	*Drab Porcelain*	? made by Lakin
Spode	1770-1833	J. LOCKETT	c. 1786-1829
		W. S. KENNEDY	1847 ——
SPODE Stone-China	pr.	J. MACINTYRE	
	cf. p. 99	MOSELEY	c. 1811-1857

MARK.	DESCRIPTION.	MARK.	DESCRIPTION.
OPERATIVE UNION POTTERY	**Burslem** 19th cent.	RILEY'S SEMI-CHINA	**Burslem** Early 19th cent.
MACHIN & POTTS *Burslem, Staffordshire*	1834	ALCOCK AND CO. HILL POTTERY BURSLEM	1826 at Cobridge. c. 1850 at Burslem
P. B. & Co.	With crown and wreath. Pinder, Bourne and Co.	S. A. & Co. ASTBURY	**Hanley** and Shelton Astbury, jun. (c. 1760-80)
	Middle 19th cent.	J. VOYEZ *Voyez Sculpt* 1769	Voyez, sculptor and potter, also worked for Wedgwood and Palmer
I. DALE. BURSLEM	c. 1800	VOYEZ & HALES, *Fecit*	c. 1780
T. & R. B.	Boote 1850-		
♂ ROGERS	Late 18th cent.- 1842		1760-78 imp.
STONE CHINA JAMES EDWARDS & CO. DALE HALL J. E. & S.	1842 onwards	H. P. NEALE & PALMER	1778-80
WALTON	1806-39		
Edge & Grocott	? Burslem 19th cent.		imp. c. 1778
ANTHONY SHAW BURSLEM	1850-		
STEEL BURSLEM	1766-1824	NEALE & WILSON Neale & Co.	1780-87

MARK.	DESCRIPTION.	MARK.	DESCRIPTION.
WILSON	**Hanley**	INDIAN STONE CHINA	**Hanley** Meigh, Old Hall Hanley 1770-1860
C WILSON	R. Wilson till 1802 D. Wilson & D. Wilson and Sons till 1820		
John Daniel, 1775			
S. Daniel, Stoke	Engraver	OPAQUE PORCELAIN	,,
Wolfe & Hamilton Stoke	c. 1790	ENAMEL PORCELAIN	,,
F. Mayer	1770-1813	SALT	c. 1820
E. Mayer & Son	1813-1830	EASTWOOD	W. Baddeley of Eastwood: 18th and early 19th cent.
Joseph Mayer & Co.	Early 19th cent.	T. SNEYD HANLEY	Early 19th cent.
T. J. & J. MAYER	c. 1830 onwards	MANN & CO. HANLEY	1857-8
MAYER BROS.	,,	KEELING, TOFT & CO.	Early 19th cent.
Mayer & Elliot	,,	JOHN RICKHUSS AND CHARLES TOFT	c. 1854
Published by C. R. BOOTH & CO. Hanley, Staffordshire	1839	S. HOLLINS	1774-1816
E I B	Birch late 18th cent.	T. & J. HOLLINS	Successors of S. Hollins
BIRCH		WARBURTON	c. 1780-1826
SHORTHOSE & HEATH	c. 1800	HACKWOOD	1842-56
SHORTHOSE & CO.	c. 1821	C. & H., Late HACKWOOD	Cookson and Harding
HEATH			

Mark.	Description.	Mark.	Description.
HARDING	**Hanley** Middle 19th cent.		**Hanley** Mason's iron- stone china was patented in 1813 pr.
FLETCHER & CO. SHELTON	1786-1810 block printers		
W. STEVENSON HANLEY	1828		
R. M. W. & Co.	Ridgway, Morley, Wear, and Co.		
Ridgway	1794 onwards		
Ridgway & Sons	1802-14		Ashworths bought up Mason's works and rights, 1859
	pr.		
	afterwards Brown, Westhead, Moore, and Co. 1855- pr.	ENOCH BOOTH 1757	**Tunstall**
G. BAGULEY, HANLEY	1810	A. & E. KEELING	Early 19th cent.
MASON'S CAMBRIAN ARGIL	Lane Delph late 18th cent.	CHILD	c. 1763
M. MASON		BOWERS	19th cent.
FENTON STONE WORKS C. J. M. & Co.	C. J. Mason and Co. 1825-51. The words "Granite China" and a view of the works also occur with this mark.		pr.

MARK.	DESCRIPTION.	MARK.	DESCRIPTION.
ADAMS	**Tunstall** 1787 onwards	*W. Greatbatch Lane Delf*	**Lane End** 1778
W. ADAMS & SON			
W. A. & S.		*Radford*	Engraver (cf. p. 104)
W. A. & Co.			A feather in a crown and word CAMBRIA on a ribbon accompany this mark early 19th cent.
MARSHALL & CO. 6	Early 19th cent.	C. HEATHCOTE & CO.	
	Hilditch and Son early 19th cent. pot. and porc.	MYATT	c. 1800
		T. Harley, Lane End	c. 1800
A. STEVENSON WARRANTED STAFFORDSHIRE	19th cent.	HARLEY	
HALL	Early 19th cent.	*Aynsley, Lane End*	c. 1790
T. GREEN	**Fenton** c. 1835	*Lane End*	
S. GREENWOOD	1770-80	*B. Plant, Lane End*	Late 18th cent.
PRATT	c. 1800 onwards	BAILEY & BATKIN	c. 1815
F. and R. PRATT & CO. FENTON		M. & N. 264 *May^r & Newbd*	Early 19th cent.
TURNER	**Lane End** 1762-1803		
W. & J. TURNER	Prince of Wales' feathers also added to this mark	CYPLES	c. 1786
TURNER & CO.			
J. MIST, 82 FLEET ST., LONDON	London agent	CHEATHAM & WOOLLEY	Early 19th cent.

Mark.	Description.	Mark.	Description.
Thomas Wooley	**Lane End** inc.	JONES & WALLEY	**Cobridge** 1835-60
G. R. 1811		J. & R. G.	John and Robert Godwin c. 1843
	Longport 1794-1887 imp.	*Elkin, Knight & Co.*	Lane Delph 19th cent.
	pr.		**Etruria** and Burslem. Wedgwood, on red stoneware c. 1760 imp.
	pr. cf. p. 99	*Wedgwood*	On cream ware c. 1760 (The letters irregular)
		WEDGWOOD	In varying sizes from 1760 onwards
		WEDGWOOD	
		Wedgwood	
		W & B	
	1819-29		1768-80
PHILLIPS, LONGPORT	1760-19th cent.		
R. DANIEL	**Cobridge** 18th cent.		
	1802-1840 imp.	WEDGWOOD & BENTLEY	In varying sizes
		Wedgwood & Bentley	,,

Mark.	Description.	Mark.	Description.
WEDGWOOD & SONS	**Etruria** Rare mark c. 1790		**Staffordshire** (miscellaneous) Registration mark used on Minton, Copeland, and other wares from 1843-83
JOSIAH WEDGWOOD *Feb.* 2, 1805	Very rare	F. MEIR *Crystal Ware*	Tunstall c. 1842 19th cent. ? Davenport
	Various commas, dashes, numbers and single letters occur on the earlier wares		
O S X	Three letters combined at random occur after 1868		19th cent.
WEDGWOOD ETRURIA *Wedgwood Etruria*	In varying sizes c. 1840	BATTY & CO.	19th cent.
WEDGWOOD	Stencilled on porcelain 1805-15 and again after 1879	*Mohr and Smith Patentees*	,,
	Painter, 1859-75	J. CLEMENTSON *Ironstone, Tillenberg*	With a phœnix. Hanley, c. 1845
		hunt	?
	From 1891. *England* added on porcelain exported to United States pr.	DUCROZ & MILLIDGE ROYAL TERRACOTTA PORCELAIN	c. 1850 In a garter enclosing the Royal crown
WEDGWOOD		BOTT & CO.	Early 19th cent.
ENGLAND	The Wedgwood marks are nearly all stamped. A single letter indicates the year on modern wares	REGINA H. & G. *Sampson Lownds* 1786	Holland and Green, Longton after 1853 ? Tunstall

MARK.	DESCRIPTION.	MARK.	DESCRIPTION.
	Staffordshire	U.S.A.	**America**
J. Hollingshead	c. 1750	*Mr. Clarkson Crolius* 1798	Potter's Hill New York
BARKER	Fenton 18th cent. (also on Newcastle ware 19th cent.)	PAUL CUSHMAN	c. 1809 Albany, N.Y.
BAYLON	late 18th cent.	NORTON & FENTON BENNINGTON V^T	(in a circle) Vermont 1839-
S. Smith	c. 1770		
B	? Boot or Booth on lustre ware c. 1815	LYMAN FENTON & CO.	c. 1848
RAINFORTH & CO.	19th cent.	ROOKWOOD POTTERY CIN. O.	Rookwood Pottery, Cincinnati, Ohio established, 1877
PROUDMAN	,,	R. P. C. O. M. L. N.	Rookwood Pottery, Cincinnati, Ohio, Maria Longworth Nicholas
NEALE & BAILEY	Hanley see p. 108		
T. SNEYD HANLEY			,,
T. & B. GODWIN NEW WHARFE	Early 19th cent.	E. & W. BENNETT CANTON AVENUE BALTIMORE, M. D.	c. 1846
CORK & EDGE	Burslem c. 1851	STONE CHINA K. T. & K.	(and a buffalo) Knowles, Taylor, and Co., East Liverpool, Ohio, 1870-
HILLCOCK AND WALTON	"Semi-china" 19th cent.	HARKER, TAYLOR, & CO. H. P. Co.	Harker Pottery Co., East Liverpool, 1840-

MARK.	DESCRIPTION.	MARK.	DESCRIPTION.
P	**Philadelphia** Bonnin & Morris Southwark c. 1770 p. in blue : cream ware	*William Ellis Tucker China Manufacturer Philadelphia* 1828	**Philadelphia** h.p. porcelain
J. Smith *1795*	*Bucks Co.*, Pa. Joseph Smith pottery 1767-1800	*Tucker & Hulme* 1828	
H R	Henry Rondebush 1811-16 *Montgomery Co. ·Pa.*	*Jo^s Hemphill* *W* **W** *m*	1832-36 workman's marks inc. Walker Morgan
Henry Roudebuth	,,	*F*	Frederick
		H	Hand
S T	Samuel Troxel 1823-33 graffiato pottery	*V*	Vivian
		CB	C. J. Boulter
G H	Georg Hübener graffiato pottery 1785-98	*Smith, Fife, & Co. Manufacturers, Phil^a*	Porc. c. 1830
IT	I. Taney *Bucks Co.* c. 1794	RALPH B. BEECH PATENTED JUNE 3, 1851 KENSINGTON, PA.	**Kensington**, Pa.
Johan Drey 1889	Johan Drey	AM. POTTERY MANUF^G CO. JERSEY CITY	**Jersey City**, N.J. (on a flag) pr. 1833-
		D. & J. *Henderson, Jersey City*	In a circle c. 1829
A H *PM*	Initials of potters in Pennsylvania		American Porcelain Manufacturing, Co.
		A. P. M. & Co.	**Gloucester**, N.J. 1854-57
H.T. IS.T.	*Montgomery Co.* J. Scholl, of Tyler's Port c. 1830 a fuchsia imp.	MERCER POTTERY TRENTON, N.J.	**Trenton**, N.J. semi-porcelain 1868-

MARK.	DESCRIPTION.	MARK.	DESCRIPTION.
BISHOPS WALTHAM	**Hants** on terra cotta 1862-66		Marks of decorators of Lancastrian pottery. Lewis F. Day (designer)
CROSSLEY COMMONDALE	**Yorks** on terra cotta 1880-83		John Chambers
R. W. MARTIN *Fulham*	On artistic stoneware		Richard Joyce
	Louis Marc Solon: on porcelain decorated in *pâte-sur-pâte* : at Sèvres, and after 1870 at Minton's, *Stoke-upon-Trent*		Walter Crane (designer)
			C. E. Cundall
VIII	Marks on Lancastrian lustred and *flambé* pottery made by Pilkington and Co. at **Clifton Junction** *Manchester.* VIII = 1908		Dorothy Dacre
	Mark of G. M. Forsyth		Jessie Jones
			Gwladys Rodgers
	Mark of W. S. Mycock		Annie Burton

Mark.	Description.	Mark.	Description.
	Bernard Moore. Stoke-upon-Trent Staffs. on Flambé glazed ware		Wileman and Co. Foley Potteries Longton, Staffs.
	Ridgway. Shelton, Staffs.		E. J. D. Bodley. Burslem, Staffs.
	Aller Vale and Watcombe Art Potteries, S. Devon. Mark also ALLER VALE		Brownfields Pottery Cobridge, Staffs.
	Royal Essex Pottery, Castle Hedingham Essex		,,
	W. Howson Taylor. Ruskin Pottery, Birmingham		J. Dimmock and Co. Hanley, Staffs.
	Torquay		Old Hall Porcelain Works Hanley, Staffs.
	Tooth and Co. Bretby Pottery near Burton-on-Trent		,,
		A. & B. ADAMS & BROMLEY	Victoria Works after 1873

Mark.	Description.	Mark.	Description.
ADAMS ENGLAND	W. Adams and Co. Tunstall Staffs.	T. B. & S.	T. and R. Boote. Burslem Staffs.
			Booths, Ltd. Tunstall Staffs.
	H. Alcock and Co. Cobridge Staffs.	O. H. BRANNAM.	Brannam. Barnstaple Devon
AYNSLEY ENGLAND	John Aynsley and Sons Longton, Staffs.	ESTABLISHED 18 R&S 50 .FOLEY CHINA.	Foley China Works Fenton, Staffs.
AULT	W. Ault. Swadlincote near Burton-on-Trent	HILL POTTERY B & L	Burgess and Leigh. Burslem Staffs.
		ENGLAND	Burslem Pottery Co. Staffs.
"Bisto."	Bishop and Stonier. Hanley, Staffs.	CAULDON ENGLAND	T. C. Brown-Westhead, Moore and Co.

MARK.	DESCRIPTION.	MARK.	DESCRIPTION.
	Cochran and Fleming. Glasgow		Doulton and Co., Ltd., Burslem.
	Doulton and Co. Lambeth		,,
	Doulton and Co., Ltd., Lambeth.		,,
	,,	ROYAL DOULTON FLAMBE	,,
	,,	DOULTON'S	,,
	,,		Elton, Sunflower Pottery Clevedon, Som.
	,,		Charles Ford. Burslem, Staffs.
			Th. Forester and Sons. Longton, Staffs.

MARK.	DESCRIPTION.	MARK.	DESCRIPTION.
	Furnivals, Ltd. Cobridge, Staffs.		Lovatt and Lovatt near Nottingham
	W. H. Goss. Stoke-upon-Trent Staffs.		J. Macintyre and Co., Burslem, Staffs.
	W. H. Grindley and Co. Tunstall		
	G. Jones and Sons. Stoke-upon-Trent Staffs.		A. Meakin, Ltd. Tunstall, Staffs.
	Locke and Co. Worcester		J. and G. Meakin. Hanley, Staffs.

Mark.	Description.	Mark.	Description.
A ⚓ †	**Bow** A in blue anchor, etc. in red.	⚓ *D*	Derby-Chelsea See p. 96
T	imp. ? Tebo	DUESBURY LONDON	**Derby** late 18th cent.
F E	in red and blue on figures	B	**Bristol** p. 95
O	inc.	H	**Lowestoft** p. 98
⚓† ☽	in red with crescent in blue	*J Hughes fecit*	on transfer print ? Liverpool p. 98
S *Salopian*	**Coalport** on the same piece	N 10 A	**Pinxton** in red
C.B.DALE	See p. 96	P	imp.
C Dale		☾ ✳	in puce
C T⊙ S⁺	? Tebo	*Rockingham* *Brameld* *Manufacturers to the* *King*	**Rockingham** pr. in pink p. 99
D L	**? Chelsea** inc.	*Or ℓ'*	inc. on a figure
S D	Derby inc.	*Brameld* 200 ✗	inc.
D	inc. on a Derby jug	*New Hall* *Shelton* BOYLE	**New Hall** 1799 p. in colour Stoke-upon-Trent c. 1830 imp.

Mark.	Description.	Mark.	Description.
G	? Church Gresley c. 1800 inc.	*Flight*	**Worcester** 1783-93 (See p. 101)
Anchors	**Worcester** on blue printed ware, c. 1770	*F x B*	Flight & Barr inc.
	Workmen's marks. Wall period (1751-83) p. in blue	*E. Doe Worcester*	on Chamberlain's Worcester Early 19th cent.
		Grainger Wood & Co. Worcester Warranted 228	Grainger's Worcester (p. 101)
	p. in black and blue	*I. Dawson & Co., Low Ford*	**Hylton** Early 19th cent. pr.
N D M	p. and inc.	J & P	**Newcastle** Jackson & Patterson Early 19th cent.
P T T	? Tebo inc.	WALLACE & CO. J. W. & CO.	late 19th cent.
T T°	p. in blue	PATTERSON & CO.	
W. P. C	p. in pink	*I. Warburton N. on Tyne*	,,
X 1757 O^s		*Tyne Pottery*	1740-1817
D	John Donaldson's signature	HARWOOD STOCKTON	**Stockton-on-Tees** late 19th cent.
R. H fecit *R. H. f* *J Ross sculp*	R. Hancock printed ware ,,	W S Jun & Co TEES	William Smith See p. 102

MARK.	DESCRIPTION.	MARK.	DESCRIPTION.
SEWELL	imp. See p. 102	EVANS & GLASSON SWANSEA	**Swansea** 1850 —— pr. in triangular form
Dixon Co.			
Dixon, Phillips & Co.		*Smith Lambeth*	Early 19th cent. stoneware
TWIGG	Kilnhurst, near Rotherham 1839 onwards	W. GREEN VAUXHALL *London*	Early 19th cent.
SOWTER & Cº MEXBRO'	late 18th cent.	WH	painter on saltglaze ? Willem Horlogius
Swillington Bridge Pottery J. Wildblood		*John Toft*	Inc. on saltglaze
Yates LEEDS	on early 19th cent. porcelain	W	p. on saltglaze ? Wedgwood
		Wolfe W	**Stoke-upon-Trent** c. 1840
Nottingham Oct. the 22 1702	inc.	*Spode's Imperial*	See p. 107
			Burslem
H. P.^{2} 1808	? Herculaneum imp.	E. WOOD *sculpt.* E. HEWITT *Pinxt.*	on a figure
JOSEPH THOMPSON WOODEN BOX POTTERY DERBYSHIRE	The Hartshorne Potteries 1818 onwards	E. WOOD & SONS	See p. 107
		WOOD	
John Milsom Maker 124 Temple Street Bristol 1830	imp. on brown stoneware		? J. Lockett (p. 107). inc.
BRADLEY & Cº COALPORT	c. 1800 ? agents	STUBBS.	Dale Hall 1790-1829 imp.

MARK.	DESCRIPTION.	MARK.	DESCRIPTION.
BATHWELL GOODFELLOW	**Burslem** c. 1800-1819 imp.	J & W RIDGWAY	**Hanley**
E. CHALLINOR	succeeded the above in 1819	W. RIDGWAY & CO	See p. 110
Joseph Edge 1760	on red ware ? Burslem	CAULDON	,,
		CAULDON PLACE ENGLAND	,,
H. & A	Hailes & Adams late 18th cent.	GLASS, HANLEY	c. 1830
	Wilson See p. 109	*W. Clowes*	Port Hill, c. 1810
		B. ADAMS	Early 19th cent.
		BOURNE NIXON & C⁰ 1830	Tunstall
HAMILTON STOKE	1818——		
T. MAYER LONGPORT	with printed cartouche and crest (a horse) c. 1830		John Yates Fenton, c. 1830
COURTHOPE	Early 19th cent.	CYPLES & BARKER	Longton, c. 1800
JOHNSON HANLEY *Stone-China*	19th cent. pr. in blue	B	Barlow (successor of the above)
William Heath	Early 19th cent. imp.	*Martin, Shaw & Cope Improved China*	in a cartouche, Longton Early 19th cent.
T. H. & CO	? T. Heath & Co.	*Carey's Saxon Stone*	Fenton. c. 1845 imp.
INDIAN TREE J. M. & CO.	J. Meigh & Sons c. 1861		
TOFT & MAY	Hanley, c. 1830	T. HEATH BURSLEM	printer early 19th cent.
HAWLEY	Foley, 1842——	*E. & G. Phillips* LONGPORT	in a wreath Early 19th cent.

Mark.	Description.	Mark.	Description.
R. HALL	Sytch pottery Burslem	MARE	c. 1830 imp.
I. HALL & SONS	Early 19th cent. imp.		
Turner's-Patent C	Lane End (See p. 99) pr. in blue	G TAYLOR	Hanley 1786-1802
		WHITENING 1.	19th cent.
R.S.	*Cobridge* imp.	B. W. & Co	Bates, Walker & Co.
STEVENSON	(see p. 112)	GILDEA & WALKER	Late 19th cent.
R STEVENSON & WILLIAMS	pr. in blue		**? Wincanton** delft c. 1720 See p. 104
Published by E. JONES COBRIDGE *September 1, 1838*	imp.	WD 4	
		g	Ireson (Wincanton) p. 104
ETRUSCAN E K B	Elkin, Knight and Bridgwood at Foley c. 1820-50		**Burslem** Rebus mark of Ralph Wood (see p. 107)
KNIGHT ELKIN &CO IRONSTONE CHINA C	pr. in blue		
J. CLEMENTSON *Bread Street* SHELTON NOVEMBER 5th 1839	pr.	W.SUCKERS	Cane ware c. 1820
I. Theophilus Stringfellow made this puzzle jug 1816	Inscribed	R S	R. Stevenson Cobridge (see p. 112)

Mark.	Description.	Mark.	Description.
	Bow incised (see p. 95)	LLOYD SHELTON	**Staffordshire** imp. c. 1820
	Derby W. Duesbury & Co. c. 1756 incised (see p. 97)	DILLWYN & CO.	**Swansea** imp. (see p. 100)
	Coalport p. in blue (see p. 96)	BEVINGTON	pr. in red after 1817

PERSIA, SYRIA, ASIA MINOR
AND EGYPT

THE pottery of the Near East, while embracing many kinds of earthenware, is usually characterised by a friable body of sandy texture: this is occasionally coated with tin-enamel, oftener with white "slip," though it is sometimes decorated directly on the body. Painting in blue and brown, turquoise and green, or in lustre pigments was practised from very early times, and the ware, except when tin-enamelled, has a translucent glaze of remarkable depth and quality. It appears probable that Egypt was the nursery of the art after the fall of the Roman Empire and in the early Middle Ages, and that its practice spread thence into Syria, Persia, and Asia Minor, where brilliant and attractive types of pottery were made from the eleventh to the seventeenth century. The rubbish mounds which cover the site of Fostat (Old Cairo) have proved rich mines of fragments and waste pieces of pottery evidently thrown away from kilns—many of which bear marks; some of the marks show that Persian and Syrian potters, or their descendants, were working in Egypt alongside the native Egyptians. Indeed the most common name *Ghaïby* signifies "stranger," and is qualified on one piece with the further description *El Châmy*, "the Syrian." The dates of these marked fragments range from the ninth to the seventeenth century.

Lustre pigments were used with great skill in Mesopotamia and Persia from the ninth to the seventeenth century, and also in Egypt about the same time. Under Turkish rule, from the sixteenth century onwards, a particularly beautiful pottery of the same type was made in Asia Minor and at Damascus. This ware, formerly known as Rhodian and Damascus ware, is noted for its brilliant colours and its decorative schemes of semi-naturalistic flowers—pinks, hyacinths, marigolds, roses, fritillaries,

etc.   A large proportion of this ware, exclusive of that known as
" Damascus," is distinguished by the use of a fine red pigment,
always in palpable relief.   This pigment, generally known as
" Rhodian red," was obtained from Armenian bole.

Marked examples of Persian, Syrian and Turkish wares are
uncommon.

A translucent pottery, which is generally known as Persian
porcelain, was made at a very early date, and then again about
1600 and even as late as 1800.   This ware frequently bears
delicately incised patterns or is ornamented with pierced patterns
the openings of which are filled with glaze.   It was formerly
known in England as " Gombroon Ware."

The marks found on Persian pottery occur most frequently on
the wares of the sixteenth to the nineteenth century, particularly
on the pieces in which Chinese influence is apparent in the
decoration.   Marks also occur on Anatolian wares of minor
importance.

MARK.	DESCRIPTION.	MARK.	DESCRIPTION.
غيبي	Ghaïby (= stranger) 16th cent. one of his pieces also bears the words El Châmy, meaning the Syrian	عمل الهرمزي	El Hermizi (= from Hormuz in Persia) 16th cent.
غيبي	,,	عمل المهرزي	,,
ع	,,	عمل المهرمزي	El Masry. Egyptian 13th or 14th cent.
غيبي	Son of Ghaïby	عمل الشامي	El Châmy, Syrian 14th cent. and later
عجمي	Aagami (= Persian) 16th cent.	عمل الشنا كي	,,
		عمل السوريزري	El Taurizi (= from Tauris) 16th cent.
		ح ح	Mark on 14th cent. ware
غزال	Ghazal 16th cent. Syrian style		Aioub 13th or 14th cent. Egyptian
الغزال	,,		Bism 16th and 17th cent. Syrian style

MARK.	DESCRIPTION.	MARK.	DESCRIPTION.
الكائى	El Chaer 16th cent. Egyptian	عمل بزرق اص	Charaf
الاا	El Siouaz 16th cent. Syrian	ابوالس	Abou-l-iizz 17th cent. Egyptian
الصوو		ابولس	Abolo 17th cent. Egyptian
حمد لذ نسنا	El Istaz, 13th or 14th cent. Persian	رح م	Aahmad. Egyptian
عمل	El Maallem 15th or 16th cent. Egyptian		Rikk. Style of Damascus
المحدثه		فتح	Fathh : style of Damascus 16th cent.
مسلم	El Mouslem on ? 9th cent. lustred ware Egyptian		
زنا ش	Nakkach 15th or 16th cent. Syrian style	العلا	Kallass. Syrian style
عمل الراح	El Barrany 13th cent. Egyptian	مال.	Tal : 16th or 17th cent. Egyptian
عمل الفقد	El Fakid 16th cent. Syrian style		

MARK.	DESCRIPTION.	MARK.	DESCRIPTION.
	Persian blue and white faïence, 16th or 17th cent., imitation of a Chinese seal		= " Belonging to Ahmed. Made by Muhammed Ali A.H. 1232 " (=A.D. 1817)
	Persian " porcelain " p. in lustre 16th or 17th cent.		=? " Made by Muhammed Harbaty "
	" Signature of Hatim		Blue and white Persian, 19th cent.
	= " The decorator of it the poor Zari A.H. 1025 " (=A.D. 1616) on blue and white faïence		"
	" = " The work of Mahmûd Mi'mar of Yezd "		"
	17th Persian resembling a Chinese mark		"
	19th cent. Persian		**Turkish** faïence 16th cent.
	= " Made by Muhammed Ali A.H. 1234 " (=A.D. 1819) On " Gombroon " ware		**Anatolian** faïence 17th cent.
			Mark of Youaz 18th cent.

CHINESE PORCELAIN

IT seems probable from literary evidence that porcelain was made in China in the sixth century: it was certainly made during the T'ang dynasty (618-906 A.D.). The various makes of the Sung (960-1279) and Yüan (1280-1367) dynasties are distinguished by monochrome glazes of great delicacy and beauty, the best known being the creamy white ware of Ting-chou and the grey green celadon of Lung-ch'üan. Marks on these wares appear to have been unusual, though the Chün-chou porcelain was sometimes marked with an engraved numeral, and a palace mark of the Yüan dynasty (*Shu fu*) is given on p. 149. Under the Ming dynasty (1368-1644 A.D.), the Yung-lo period (1403-24) was celebrated for its fine white porcelain with white traceries beneath the glaze; the Hsüan-tê period (1426-35) for blue and white (*i.e.* white porcelain painted in underglaze blue) and a brilliant underglaze red decoration; the Ch'êng-hua period (1465-1487) for coloured decoration, painted in enamels and in glazes; the Hung-chih period (1488-1505) for a pale transparent yellow; the Chia-ching period (1522-66) for blue and white; the Lung-ch'ing (1567-72) and Wan-li (1573-1619) periods for enamelled decoration combined with underglaze blue, principally in five colours, including green, yellow, manganese purple and red. Genuine specimens of Ming porcelain made before the sixteenth century are still rare, though the marks of Hsüan-tê and Ch'êng-hua occur very commonly on comparatively modern wares.

The reigns of K'ang-hsi (1662-1722), Yung-chêng (1723-35) and Ch'ien-lung (1736-95) have supplied the bulk of the finest Chinese porcelain in European collections. The K'ang-hsi period is noted for the perfection of blue and white porcelain; enamelled porcelains in three and five colours,[1] with a predominance of green in various shades, whence the French name *famille verte*; porcelain with coloured grounds, *e.g.* greenish-black, powder-blue, coral-red, coffee-brown, leaf-green, etc., and reserved decoration in other colours ; single-coloured wares with glazes of *sang de bœuf* red, peach-bloom, apple-green, and other tints. The reign of Yung-chêng (1723-35) was noted for the clever imitations of the ancient wares of the Sung dynasty with single-coloured, splashed, and crackled glazes. Indeed most of the archaic-looking specimens in our collections, with glazes of this description, were made about this time. Among enamels the various rose tints which came into use at the end of the preceding reign, were fully developed ; and this period marks the transition of the *famille verte* into the *famille rose,* the old translucent enamels of limited range being replaced by an extended palette of opaque colours. The elaborately and minutely painted "egg-shell" plates and services (often with ruby-red ground underneath) were decorated at Canton mainly for export ; and from this time onward large consignments of porcelain decorated to order with crests and coats of arms were shipped to Europe. The porcelain itself was made, like nearly all the Chinese porcelain known to us, at Ching-tê-chên,[2] in the province of Kiangsi, but the enamelled decoration in Western taste was added in Canton.

During the long reign of Ch'ien-lung (1736-95) mechanical perfection was reached in the manufacture of porcelain. There was little, old or new, that the potters could not achieve. Their glazes imitated jade, bronze, carved wood, lacquer, natural stones, and all kinds of ornamental materials ; and many new glaze colours were adopted, *e.g. soufflé* red of coral tint, deep sapphire blue (known as the "Temple of Heaven" blue), "iron-rust" and "tea-dust" glazes. The painted wares are wonders of manipulative skill, though their delicate and elaborate finish may not be so pleasing as the bolder style and broader effects of the K'ang-hsi porcelains. A gradual but sure decline set in after the reign of Ch'ien-lung, and the nineteenth-century porcelain can usually be distinguished from the old wares by its inferior potting, weaker

---

[1] The enamels are always translucent, and at this time an overglaze enamel blue largely replaced the underglaze blue in the five-colour decoration.

[2] The principal exception to this statement is the ivory-white porcelain known in France as *blanc de Chine,* which has been made in the province of Fukien from the early part of the Ming dynasty.

colours, and comparative poverty of design.   Marks on Chinese
porcelain group themselves as follows :—(A) Date marks.   (B)
Hall marks.   (C) Marks of commendation, description, etc.
(D) Signatures.   (E) Symbols.   The inscriptions are either in
ordinary script or in seal characters (see p. 136), the ideographs
being arranged in parallel columns, read from the top, and the
columns taken from right to left.   The mark is nearly always
under the base and sometimes enclosed in a double ring, but on
some of the older specimens it occurs on the side or neck of the
vessel in a single vertical or horizontal line.   It is usually painted
in blue under the glaze ; though it also appears in red, black or
gold on the glaze, particularly on wares of the present dynasty ;
and it is sometimes stamped like a seal in the body of the ware.

(A) DATE MARKS.—Chinese dates are reckoned by two systems
of chronology—(1) Cycles of sixty years ; (2) the *nien-hao, i.e.*
arbitrary names given by the Emperors to the periods during
which they reigned.

1. *Cyclical dates* are not common and are, as a rule, incon-
clusive, because they mention only the year of the cycle without
specifying the cycle itself.   The Chinese cycles are reckoned from
B.C. 2637 ; but the table on p. 133, which begins at the 45th cycle
and ends with the 76th (*i.e.* A.D. 4 to 1923), will suffice for ceramic
purposes.   Each year of the sixty is known by a name composed
of one of the "Ten Stems" combined with one of the "twelve
Branches," which are also the names of the signs of the Zodiac.
Two examples will explain their use :—

_{1   2   3   4   5   6   6   4   5}
Wu-ch'ên nien Liang-chi shu = painting of Liang-chi in the

_{1   2   3}
Wu-ch'ên year.   The first two characters will be found to

represent the fifth year in the table, but no indication is given of
the cycle to which it belongs.   The second instance is exceptional

and the date can be guessed.   It reads Yu hsin-ch'ou nien chih =
made in the hsin-ch'ou year recurring.   The hsin-ch'ou year,
the 38th of the cycle, recurred in the reign of Kang-hsi who
completed a full cycle of his reign in A.D. 1721.

2. The commonest system of dating porcelain is by the
Nien-hao, or reign-name adopted by the Emperor on the New
Year succeeding the death of his predecessor.   These dates are
usually written in six characters in two columns ; the name of
the dynasty coming first, followed by the reign-name of the
Emperor ; the usual ending is *nien* (year or period) *chih* (made),
but the latter word is occasionally replaced by *tsao* which also

化 大
年 明
製 成

means "made" (see p. 150) *e.g.* *Ta Ming*
Ch'êng hua nien chih = made in the Ch'êng-
hua period (of the) great Ming (dynasty).
The mark is sometimes shortened into four
characters by the omission of the name of
the dynasty, (see p. 135).   The individual year
of the reign is very rarely specified.   Occasion-
ally the word *yü*, Imperial, is used instead of *nien*: (see p. 150).

The reader is cautioned that these reign-marks cannot be
accepted as true dates, without other evidence.   The Chinese,
who venerate antiquity, make a practice of putting ancient dates
on modern wares.   *Hsüan-tê* and *Ch'êng-hua* in the *Ming*
dynasty, *K'ang-hsi*, *Yung-chêng* and *Ch'ien-lung* of the *Ch'ing*
dynasty are commonly used in this way, because of the ceramic
greatness of the reigns indicated.   The exception to this caution
is the Imperial porcelain, on which the mark is accurately and
skilfully inscribed.

The following tables include the principal reign-names of the
Ming and *Ch'ing* dynasties, marks previous to these being
virtually unknown, although they are reputed to have been first
placed on Imperial wares by order of the Emperor Chên-tsung in
the period *Ching-tê* (1004-7 A.D.).   From the reign of *Yung
Chêng* onwards seal characters were commonly used in the reign-
marks, as shown below.   A list of Chinese numerals is appended.

(B) HALL MARK.—The term "hall" here used is vague but
comprehensive.   It may refer to the shed of the potter, the
studio of the painter, the shop of a dealer, the hall of a noble

or the palace or pavilion of an Emperor.   It may equally signify
the place where, or the place for which the ware was made ; and
in the absence of any preposition the meaning of the hall-mark
must often remain obscure.   The word used in those marks is
usually *t'ang*, a hall (see p. 142) ; but *t'ing*, a summer-house also
occurs, as well as *chai*, a studio (p. 144), *hsüan*, a terrace (p. 151),
and *fang*, a retreat (p. 143).

(C) MARKS OF COMMENDATION, etc., include (1) laudatory
terms such as *Pao shêng* (of unique value) on p. 147, "a gem
among precious vessels of rare jade" (p. 146), etc., referring to the
beauty of the ware ; (2) words of good omen such as *Shou*
(longevity), *Fu* (happiness), etc., implying a wish for the welfare
of the owner of the vessel ; and (3) inscriptions which refer to the
subject of the decoration, *e.g. Tsai ch'uan chih lo* = "Feeling pleasure in the water," the subject being fishes in a pool (see below).

(D) SIGNATURES are rare on Chinese porcelain, chiefly because
of the minute division of labour in the factories, where one
piece sometimes passed through seventy hands.   Some of the
"hall marks," however, must be regarded as containing "studio
names" of potters or decorators, and therefore as a kind of
signature.

(E) SYMBOLS, DEVICES, etc., so dear to the Chinese mind, are
often found in place of a written mark, the commonest being the
Eight Buddhist symbols, the attributes of the Taoist Immortals,
the Hundred Antiques, and Emblems of Happiness or Long-life
such as the bat and the fungus.   More rarely a group of objects
can be translated rebus-fashion into a good wish ; *e.g.* a pencil-
brush (*pi*) with a cake of ink (*ting*) and a (*ju-i*) sceptre or magic
wand, together connote the phrase *Pi ting ju-i*, "May (things) be
fixed as you wish" (p. 141).

In the year 1667 the Emperor K'ang-hsi forbade the use of
the Imperial title or any sacred phrase on china, lest it should
be broken and desecrated.   It is unlikely that the prohibition
remained in force for more than a few years, but during that
time the double ring intended to enclose the mark either
remained blank or was filled with a device or symbol or some
other permissible substitute.

chih   知   在   tsai

lo   樂   川   ch'uan

= feeling pleasure in the water.

CHINESE POTTERY

THE manufacture of pottery in China is of immemorial antiquity, but its history prior to the Han dynasty (B.C. 206–A.D. 220) is chiefly of antiquarian interest. At this time it appears from literary evidence that stoneware, a very hard and partially vitrified pottery, was made ; and from actual existing specimens that a red earthenware with green or brown glaze was fashioned in vases of more or less artistic form, borrowed from the still more ancient bronzes. The spread of tea-drinking during the T'ang dynasty (A.D. 618-906) proved, no doubt, a great stimulus to the potters, but there is little marked pottery before the Ming dynasty (A.D. 1368-1644). It was in the reign of Chêng-tê (1506-1521) that the potteries of Yi-hsing-hsien, in the province of Kiangsu, were started. The Yi-hsing ware is an unglazed pottery of varying hardness, and usually of red, buff, or fawn colours. It was called by the Portuguese "buccaro," and is best known in tea-pots of fantastic shapes, such as Böttger of Dresden, certain Dutch potters, and Dwight and Elers in England copied at the end of the seventeenth and the beginning of the eighteenth centuries. The later examples are often enamelled and the manufacture continues to this day. Important stoneware factories exist in the province of Kuang-tung, dating perhaps from the Sung dynasty (A.D. 960-1279), but best known to us by their later products, *e.g.* jars, vases, and figures with splashed and mottled glazes with a prevailing blue or bluish grey tone streaked and flecked with scarlet, green, and olive brown. There are potteries near Peking producing good copies of the porcelain with turquoise and aubergine glazes, and there are many obscure factories which supply local needs ; but the marked Chinese pottery in European hands can, as a rule, be safely assigned to either a Yi-hsing or Canton origin.

Marks on Chinese pottery usually consist of impressed seals giving the name (or art-name) of the potter or place of manufacture ; and date-marks are uncommon.

Cyclical Signs		CYCLE BEGINNING					Cyclical Signs		CYCLE BEGINNING				
		A.D. 4	A.D. 64	A.D.	A.D.	A.D.			A.D. 4	A.D. 64	A.D.	A.D.	A.D.
		304	364	124	184	244			304	364	124	184	244
		604	664	424	484	544			604	664	424	484	544
		904	964	724	784	844			904	964	724	784	844
		1204	1264	1024	1084	1144			1204	1264	1024	1084	1144
		1504	1564	1324	1384	1444			1504	1564	1324	1384	1444
		1804	1864	1624	1684	1744			1804	1864	1624	1684	1744
甲 子		04	64	24	84	44	甲 午		34	94	54	14	74
乙 丑		05	65	25	85	45	乙 未		35	95	55	15	75
丙 寅		06	66	26	86	46	丙 申		36	96	56	16	76
丁 卯		07	67	27	87	47	丁 酉		37	97	57	17	77
戊 辰		08	68	28	88	48	戊 戌		38	98	58	18	78
己 巳		09	69	29	89	49	己 亥		39	99	59	19	79
庚 午		10	70	30	90	50	庚 子		40	100	60	20	80
辛 未		11	71	31	91	51	辛 丑		41	101	61	21	81
壬 申		12	72	32	92	52	壬 寅		42	102	62	22	82
癸 酉		13	73	33	93	53	癸 卯		43	103	63	23	83
甲 戌		14	74	34	94	54	甲 辰		44	104	64	24	84
乙 亥		15	75	35	95	55	乙 巳		45	105	65	25	85
丙 子		16	76	36	96	56	丙 午		46	106	66	26	86
丁 丑		17	77	37	97	57	丁 未		47	107	67	27	87
戊 寅		18	78	38	98	58	戊 申		48	108	68	28	88
己 卯		19	79	39	99	59	己 酉		49	109	69	29	89
庚 辰		20	80	40	100	60	庚 戌		50	110	70	30	90
辛 巳		21	81	41	101	61	辛 亥		51	111	71	31	91
壬 午		22	82	42	102	62	壬 子		52	112	72	32	92
癸 未		23	83	43	103	63	癸 丑		53	113	73	33	93
甲 申		24	84	44	104	64	甲 寅		54	114	74	34	94
乙 酉		25	85	45	105	65	乙 卯		55	115	75	35	95
丙 戌		26	86	46	106	66	丙 辰		56	116	76	36	96
丁 亥		27	87	47	107	67	丁 巳		57	117	77	37	97
戊 子		28	88	48	108	68	戊 午		58	118	78	38	98
己 丑		29	89	49	109	69	己 未		59	119	79	39	99
庚 寅		30	90	50	110	70	庚 申		60	120	80	40	100
辛 卯		31	91	51	111	71	辛 酉		61	121	81	41	101
壬 辰		32	92	52	112	72	壬 戌		62	122	82	42	102
癸 巳		33	93	53	113	73	癸 亥		63	123	83	43	103

CHINESE DATE MARKS

Nienhao of the Emperors on Porcelain and Pottery

MARK.	DESCRIPTION.	MARK.	DESCRIPTION.
	Wu fêng êrh nien = second year of Wu Fêng, i.e. 56 B.C.		**Sung dynasty** Yüan Fêng (1078-85)
	Yung p'ing yüan nien tsao = made in the first year of Yung P'ing, i.e. 58 A.D.		**Ming dynasty** Hung Wu (1368-98)
			Yung Lo (1403-24)
			The same in archaic script
	Sung dynasty Ching Tê (1004-7)		Hsiian Tê (1426-35)
	Hsi Ning (1068-77)		The same in seal characters

MARK.	DESCRIPTION.	MARK.	DESCRIPTION.
化年製 大明成 成化	**Ming dynasty** Ch'êng Hua (1465-87) The same	曆年製 大明萬	**Ming dynasty** Wan Li (1573-1619)
成化年製	The same in seal characters	啟年製 大明天	T'ien Ch'i (1621-27)
治年製 大明弘 德年製	Hung Chih (1488-1505)	年製 崇禎 大清順 治年製	Ch'ung Chêng (1628-44) **Ch'ing dynasty** Shun Chih (1644-61)
大明正	Chêng Tê (1506-21)		The same in seal characters
靖年製 大明嘉	Chia Ching (1522-66)	熙年製 大清康	K'ang Hsi (1662-1722)
慶年製 大明隆	Lung Ch'ing (1567-72)		The same in seal characters

MARK.	DESCRIPTION.	MARK.	DESCRIPTION.
大清雍正年製	**Ch'ing dynasty** Yung Chêng (1723-35)	大清豐年製 (seal)	**Ch'ing dynasty** Tao Kuang (1821-50)
大清雍正年製 (seal)	The same in seal characters	大清咸豐年製	Hsien Fêng (1851-61)
大清乾隆年製	Ch'ien Lung (1736-95)	大清咸豐年製 (seal)	The same in seal characters
(seal)	The same in seal characters	大清同治年製	T'ung Chih (1862-74)
(seal)	,,	大清同治年製 (seal)	The same in seal characters
大清嘉慶年製	Chia Ch'ing (1796-1820)	大清光緒年製	Kuang Hsü 1875-1908
大清嘉慶年製 (seal)	The same in seal characters	大清光緒年製 (seal)	The same in seal characters
大清道光年製	Tao Kuang (1821-50)	大清宣統年製	Hsüan T'ung 1909-12

CHINESE NUMERALS

	Common	Short	Long	
1	一	｜	壹	Yi
2	二	｜｜	貳	Erh
3	三	｜｜｜	叁	San (rare)
4	四	╳	肆	Ssŭ
5	五	８	伍	Wu
6	六	⊥	陸	Liu
7	七	╧	柒	Ch'i
8	八	╪	捌	Pa
9	九	夂	玖	Chiu
10	十		拾	Shih

These Chinese numerals will assist in calculating those rare Chinese and Japanese dates in which a particular year, month, or day is specified. Three forms are given: the common form on the left, the short form in the middle; and the long form on the right. Chinese numerals of the common form were used as marks on the Chün-chou porcelain of the Sung dynasty (960-1279 A.D.).

The numerals in Japanese read :—1. Ichi. 2. Futatsu or Ni. 3. San. 4. Yotsu or Shi. 5. Itsutsu. 6. Mutsu or Roku. 7. Nanatsu or Shichi. 8. Yatsu or Hachi. 9. Kokohotsu or Ku. 10. Ju or To.

MARK.	DESCRIPTION.	MARK.	DESCRIPTION.
	The Eight Precious Things (Pa Pao) Chu (a jewel)		**The Eight Buddhist Emblems (Pa Chi-hsiang)** Chêng (a bell). Sometimes the wheel (lun) is substituted for the bell
	Ch'ien ("a cash")		Lo (a conch shell)
	Fang-shêng (a lozenge, symbol of victory)		San (State umbrella)
	Hua (a painting)		Kai (canopy)
	Ch'ing (a hanging musical stone of jade)		Lien Hua (lotus flower)
	Shu (a pair of books)		P'ing (vase)
	Chüeh (a pair of rhinoceros horn cups)		Yü (a pair of fishes)
	Ai-yeh (an artemisia leaf)		Chang (entrails) an endless knot

MARK.	DESCRIPTION.	MARK.	DESCRIPTION.
	A hare looking at the moon. K'ang-hsi period (1662-1722)		Lotus flower
	A hare (T'u). Late Ming and K'ang-hsi periods		,,
	,, The hare which lives in the moon making the elixir of life, is venerated by the Taoists		Flowers
	Artemisia leaf : a good omen		Prunus spray (Mei hua)
	,,		Fungus (Lingchih) Emblem of Longevity
	Lotus flower		,,
			A bat and two peaches (Fu shou Shuang ch'üan) a rebus = "Happiness and longevity both complete"

MARK.	DESCRIPTION.	MARK.	DESCRIPTION.
	Flower		A four-legged incense burner
	,,		A tripod incense burner
	,,		A tripod vase
	Head of a ju-i sceptre (of Longevity)		A tailless stork.
	Endless knot		Marks engraved on specimens in the Dresden collection :—zigag, on blue and white :
	Insect	*N=665,*	cross on Japanese wares : H, on Chinese famille verte : triangle, on white Chinese : arrow, on red Chinese : parallelogram on "Old Indian" porcelain
	Four-legged incense burner (Ting) See p. 97	*N=50*	

MARK.	DESCRIPTION.	MARK.	DESCRIPTION.
	Fu (one of the 12 ancient embroidery ornaments)		Lozenge symbol
	Pearl symbol		Pair of books
	Shell symbol		Cash symbol
	Pearl symbol		Two fishes, emblem of felicity
	? Musical instruments		,,
	Lozenge symbol		,,
	Swastika symbol or fylfot, in a lozenge		Perhaps rhinoceros horn cups
	Lozenge symbol		A brush (pi) a cake of ink (ting) and a sceptre of longevity (ju-i), making the rebus Pi ting ju i = " May (things) be fixed as you wish ! "

MARK.	DESCRIPTION.	MARK.	DESCRIPTION.
佳器 玉堂 堂製 永樂	Yü t'ang chia ch'i = beautiful vessel for the jade hall. Late Ming and early Ch'ing dynasties	致遠 堂製	Chih yüan t'ang chih = made at the hall of wide extension. 1736-95
	Yung lo t'ang chih = made at the Yung lo (perpetual enjoyment hall) c. 1730	敬畏 堂製	Ching wei t'ang chih = made for the hall of respectful awe. A palace mark 1736-95
堂製 彩華	Ts'ai hua t'ang chih = made at the hall of brilliant painting. 1820-50	德馨 堂製 棻 猗 堂	Tê hsing t'ang chih = made for the hall of fragrant virtue. 1573-1620
	Chih hao t'ang ch'ing shang = pure gift from the hall of good endeavour. 1821-50		Lu i t'ang = Hall of green ripples : 18th cent.
彩秀 堂製	Ts'ai hsiu t'ang chih = made at the hall of brilliant decorations. 1821-50	玉海 堂製	Yü hai t'ang chih = made in the hall of ocean jade. 1662-1722
交子 堂製	Yu tzŭ t'ang chih = made for the hall of friends and scholars. 1662-1722	慎德 堂製	Shên tê t'ang chih = made for the hall of cultivation of virtue. Palace mark 1820-50

MARK.	DESCRIPTION.	MARK.	DESCRIPTION.
慎德堂製	Shên tê t'ang po ku chih = antique made at the Shên-tê hall, 1820-50	林玉堂製	Lin yü t'ang chih = made at the hall of abundant jade. 1662-1722
聚順美彩潤益右大樹奇玉	Chü shun mei yü t'ang chih = made at the Chü shun hall of beautiful jade. late 17th cent.	景濂堂倣古製	Ching lien t'ang fang ku chih = imitations of antiques made at the Chinglien hall. late 18th cent.
博古製玉堂製堂製堂製堂製堂製	Ts'ai jun t'ang chih = made at the hall of brilliant colours. early 19th cent.	養和堂製	Yang ho t'ang chih = made at the hall for the cultivation of harmony. 1723-35
	I yu t'ang chih = made at the hall of ? prosperity and profit. ? 17th cent.	瑞麓山房監製	Jui lu shan fang chien chih = made in the mountain dwelling under the superintendence of Jui-lu. 1662-1722
	Ta shu t'ang chih = made at the big tree hall. 1820-50	芝蘭製	Chih lan chai chih = made in the epidendrum studio. 17th cent.
	Ch'i yü t'ang chih = made at the hall of rare jade. 1662-1722	詹寧齋製	Tan ning chai chih = made in the pavilion of peace and tranquillity. 1736-95

MARK.	DESCRIPTION.	MARK.	DESCRIPTION.
	Ssŭ pu chai chih = made for the pavilion of meditation for the correction of faults. ? early 18th cent.		Yung ch'ing ch'ang ch'un = Eternal prosperity and enduring spring !
	Kuei yüeh shan chuang = workshop of the Cassia Moon Mountain. 1820-50		T'ien ti yi chia ch'un = Springtime in heaven and earth—one family. (Motto of the late Empress Dowager) and Ta Ya Chai = Pavilion of grand culture : (one of her palaces) late 19th cent.
	Jo shên chên ts'ang = to be treasured like a gem from the deep. 18th and 19th cent.		Ssŭ yu mei yü ya chih = thoughts elegantly expressed in beautiful jade. 1662-1722
	Shuang ch'i jo shên chên ts'ang = to be treasured like a deep gem of Shuang-ch'i. early 18th cent.		
	Ya su kung shang = For the learned and common alike to take pleasure in. early 18th cent.		Ta chi = Great good-luck !
	Hsi ch'ên ku wan = antique of the " mat jewel " (i.e. scholar) 1662-1722		Chi hsiang ju i = Good fortune and fulfilment of wishes !
	Tê hua ch'ang ch'un = Virtue culture and enduring spring ! surrounded by the date mark of Wan-li (1573-1619)		Shuang hsi = Double (or wedded) joy ! On wedding gifts

MARK.	DESCRIPTION.
	Various forms of *Shou* = longevity, the common form of which is

MARK.	DESCRIPTION.	MARK.	DESCRIPTION.
	Shou (longevity) A curious form known in Holland as the spider mark		Fu kuei chia ch'i = fine vase for the rich and honourable. 16th cent.
	Fu = happiness		Ch'ang ming fu kuei = Long life, riches, and honour! in a circle like a ''cash.'' 16th cent.
	in various forms		Ch'ing = Congratulations!
	''		Ch'i yü pao ting chih chên = A gem among precious vessels of rare jade! 1662-1722
	''		
	''		
	Lu = emolument		Ch'i shih pao ting chih chên = A gem among precious vessels of rare stone!
	An unusual form of Fu Shou = Happiness and long life!		
	Wan fu yu t'ung = May infinite happiness embrace all your affairs! 16th cent.		Ch'i chên ju yü = A gem rare as jade! 1662-1722

Mark.	Description.	Mark.	Description.
西玉友來宝勝丹桂錦玉公用雅集 南川師府聖友	Hsi yü = Western jade early 19th cent. Yu lai = Arrival of friends Pao shêng = Inexpressibly precious early 18th cent. Tan kuei = red cassia : emblem of literary honours 16th cent. Nan ch'uan chin yü = embroidered jade of Nan-ch'uan (a name for Ching-tê-chên). 1662-1722 Shuai fu kung yung = for public use in the general's hall. 17th cent. Shêng yu ya chi = Elegant collection of holy friends 1662-1722	珍賞珍玩賜祉無 愛蓮博古天官賜福萬壽疆 萬壽森疆	Ai lien chên shang = Precious reward of the lover of the lotus ! 1820-50 Po ku chên wan = a jewelled trinket of antique art T'ien kuan tz'ŭ fu = May the heavenly powers confer happiness ! Wan shou wu chiang = A myriad ages never ending ! Wan shou wu chiang = A myriad ages never ending ! Usually written in an horizontal line

MARK.	DESCRIPTION.	MARK.	DESCRIPTION.
文章 山斗	Wên chang shan tou = Scholarship lofty as the hills and the Great Bear ! 1662-1722	天	T'ien = heaven early 18th cent.
玉	Yü = jade	雅	Ya wan = elegant trinket early 18th cent.
古	Ku = antique 1662-1722	玩	
珍	Chên = a pearl 1662-1722	真玉	Chên yü = veritable jade
雅	Ya = elegant 17th cent.	玩玉	Wan yü = trinket jade
全	Ch'üan = complete 17th cent.	珍玩	Chên wan = precious trinket
聖	Shêng = holy 1662-1722	圀	? Pao (precious) or Shan wang 18th cent.
順	Shun = harmony 1662-1722	圀	? A shop mark undeciphered
興	Hsing = exalted 1662-1722		
國	Kuo = national 1662-1722		Shih fu = manifest happiness enclosed in a ground, engraved 1662-1722

MARK.	DESCRIPTION.	MARK.	DESCRIPTION.
	Fu fan chih tsao = made for the Prince of Fu (who resided in Honan 1601-1640).		Shang su (name) 1736-95
	? Lai (a name) 1662-1722		Yuan Hsin-hsing tsao = made by Yuan Hsin-hsing 19th cent.
	? Chao-chin (a name) Early 18th cent. stamped		Chang Ming kao tsao = made by Chang Ming-kao. on biscuit 1662-1722
	Chung t'un shih = Chung t'un family 18th cent. engraved		Chih = made to order (i.e. imperial)
	? Li-chih (a name) stamped 18th cent.		Fa = emitted (i.e. for sale) 1622-1722
	Lin ch'ang fa tsao = made by Lin-ch'ang fa 1736-95		Shu fu = imperial palace. On Yuan dynasty ware (1280-1367)
	Ch'ên kuo chih tsao = made by Ch'ên-kuo-chih. on biscuit 1662-1722		Baragon Tumed = Western Tumed 1820-50 (Mongolian script) Made for the princess of the west wing of the Tumed Mongolian banners

Mark.	Description.	Mark.	Description.
	Ch'a = tea		Shan jên ch'ên wei = The Hermit Ch'ên-wei ? 17th cent. inc. on white Fukien porcelain
	Chiu = wine		
	Tsao t'ang = decoction of dates (chow-chow)		
	Chiang t'ang = decoction of ginger		
	Kuan lien fang chih = made for the look-lily boat (*i.e.* excursion boat for viewing the lotus flowers) 1736-95		Hsieh chu tsao = made for the Hsieh bamboos early 19th cent.
			Hsieh chu chu jên tsao = made for the Lord of the Hsieh Bamboos early 19th cent.
	Ts'ang lang lü shui = green water of the boundless ocean 16th cent.		Kuan yao nei tsao = made at the government factory 1820-50
	Chung ch'êng fu = father "governor" (*i.e.* governor of a province)		Yung chêng yü chih = made by order of the Emperor Yung chêng (1723-35)
	Chung ch'êng = governor of a province. On copies of old crackle ware		Lien ch'êng ch'i hou Probably Lien-ch'êng is a potter's name

MARK.	DESCRIPTION.	MARK.	DESCRIPTION.
	= Made by Wang Shêng-kao at the end of the 4th month of the 3rd year of Chia-ch'ing" (*i.e.* 1798). on "rice-grain" porcelain		Yu fêng yang lin = Yang Lin of Yu fêng (a place not far from Ching-tê-chên). on an "egg-shell" plate
G	Probably a copy of the letter G (1662-1722)		Yu chai = quiet l'avilion (studio name of painter) c. 1724. on an "egg-shell" plate
	Chu shih chü = The red rocks retreat		Kung ming fu kuei Hung fu ch'i t'ien = "A famous name, riches and honour : abounding happiness reaching to heaven!" on an "egg-shell" plate c. 1724
	Wan shih chü = The myriad rocks retreat		
	Tsui yüeh hsüan chih = made on the terrace of the drunken moon c. 1800		Uncertain seal marks
	Ling nan hui chê = a Lingnan (*i.e.* Canton) painting ; and the seal Pai shih = White Rock (a studio name of a painter) c. 1724 on an "egg-shell" porcelain plate		Square seal (1662-1722) copied at Worcester
			Mark (unde-ciphered) on porcelain made for the Siamese market. 18th cent.

MARK.	DESCRIPTION.	MARK.	DESCRIPTION.
	Wu chên hsien yao = pottery of Wu-chên Hsien		**Canton** stoneware Li-ta-lai (name of a potter) Canton stoneware 18th or 19th cent.
			T'ai yüan (potter) 18th or 19th cent.
	Canton stoneware I shêng = Harmonious prosperity. on Canton stoneware		Yüch ch'ang (potter)
			Yi-hsing pottery Yi-hsing (on red stoneware of Yi-hsing-hsien, in Chang-chou-fu) 19th cent.
	Ko Ming hsiang chih = made by Ko Ming-hsiang 18th cent.		Hui mêng ch'ên chih = made by Hui Mêng-ch'ên. An old name on modern wares
	Ko yüan hsiang chih = made by Ko Yüan-hsiang 18th cent.		Mêng-ch'ên and Hui
	Huang yün chi = registered by Huang-yün 19th cent.		Yu lan pi chih = secretly made by Yu-lan
	Ch'ien yüan kai ch'ieh = Cut by Ch'ien Yuan-kai 18th cent.		Chin yüan yu chi = registered by Chin Yüan-yu 19th cent.

MARK.	DESCRIPTION.	MARK.	DESCRIPTION.
陳天遂造	Ch'ên t'ien sui tsao = made by Ch'ên T'ien-sui. K'ang Hsi period (1662-1722)	富繞吉造	Kung liang chi tsao = made by Kung Liang-chi. c. 1700
王佐廷作	Wang tso t'ing tso = made by Wang Tso-t'ing. Early 19th cent.	張家造	Chang chia tsao = made by Chang-chia. ? 16th cent.
王炳南鴻	Wang ping jung tso = made by Wang Ping-jung. Early 19th cent.	王氏壽明	Wang shih shou ning = Mr. Wang Shou-ming ? 16th cent.
陳文柏塑　萬曆丁酉	Wan li ting yu ch'ên wên Ch'êng su = Ch'ên Wên-Ch'êng modelled it in the *ting yu* year of Wan Li (1597 A.D.)	崔	Ts'ui. ? 13th cent.
		來又見	Lai Kuan 17th cent.
		芝亭	**Yi-hsing pottery** Chih ting = Sesamum pavilion 18th cent.
隻金式製　天啟乙丑	T'ien ch'i i ch'ou nien chin shih chih = made by Chin-shih in the *i-ch'ou* year of T'ien Ch'i (1625 A.D.)	德陳鳴遠	Hsiu lung tê chi = recorded by Hsiu Lung-tê Early 18th cent. Ch'ên ming yüan chih = made by Ch'ên Ming-yuan. A mid-17th century potter.

Mark.	Description.	Mark.	Description.
仁和館	Jên ho kuan = house of benevolent harmony. Sung period. (960-1279 A.D.)	湛靜齋製 軒製	Chan ching chai chih = made for the hall of profound peace. Early 19th cent.
仁存堂	Jên ts'un t'ang = hall of benevolence. ? 18th century	古月軒製	Ku yüeh hsüan chih = made on the ancient moon terrace. Early 18th cent.
堂製 三和	San ho t'ang chih = made for the hall of triple harmony. Early 19th cent.	珍藏 書屋 裕齡	Ch'ien yin shu wu ch'ên tsang = a gem to be treasured in the Ch'ien yin study. 18th cent.
玉堂	Yü t'ang chia ch'i = beautiful vessel of the jade hall. Early 17th cent.	絲 秀	Yü chüeh = surpass jade 18th cent.
尚齋堂造	Shan tso. Shang ku t'ang kung tsao = made for general use in the Shang-ku hall. Shan tso = prov. of Shantung. 18th cent.	圖 工	Shu ch'ang, i.e. made for the Shu ch'ang, a college in the Han lin University at Peking. Kung = (good) workmanship. c. 1700
堂南	Nan hsiang t'ang = south aspect hall. 18th cent.	馬臣造	Ma chên shih tsao = made by Ma Chên-shih. T'ang dynasty (618-906 A.D.)

MARK.	DESCRIPTION.	MARK.	DESCRIPTION.
年製 洪憲	Hung Hsien Nienhao adopted by Yüan Shih-k'ai in 1916	德合	**Canton** stoneware Tê ho potter's mark 19th cent.
居仁堂製	Chü jên t'ang chih = made in the Hall where Benevolence abides Hall mark of Yuan Shih-k'ai	大昌號	Ta ch'ang hao = mark of Ta-ch'ang 19th cent.
朝宗	**Fukien** Chao tsung ho yin = seal of Ho chao-tsung 17th cent.		
朝宗	Ho chao-tsung in a gourd	宜興紫砂	**Yi-hsing** pottery Yi hsing tzŭ sha = brown earth of Yi-hsing 19th cent.
	Stork mark on late Ming blue and white porcelain	德	Ming yüan 17th cent. (see p. 152A)
厚昌	**Canton** stoneware Hou ch'ang potter's mark 19th cent.		Yü lan pi chih = secretly made by Yü-lan 19th cent. (see p. 152)

JAPANESE POTTERY

THOUGH a primitive pottery was made in Japan before our era, it was not till the practice of tea-drinking necessitated a better class of ware that anything of artistic pretensions was made. In the thirteenth century Kato Shirozaemon, better known as Toshiro, journeyed to China to learn the secrets of the Chinese potters. On his return he made the first glazed wares, which consisted chiefly of tea-jars and tea-bowls of fine stoneware with rich streaky glazes, amber brown, chocolate, and purplish black, sometimes superposed. A yellow glaze was added in the next generation. These glazes, known as *Seto gusuri*, or Seto glazes, were for long the only covering for Japanese pottery. Towards the end of the sixteenth century, after the invasion of Corea, a number of Corean potters were transplanted to Japan by the victorious Hideyoshi and proved a powerful influence in Japanese ceramics. Tea-drinking became an organised cult, and the tea societies (*Chanoyu*) acquired a semi-political significance. In their ceremonies the tea-drinkers studied an almost rude simplicity, and the wares affected by them were of an archaic character, so that the potters had to devote themselves to copying the old Seto and Corean wares. The latter included wares with greyish-white glaze, or grey stoneware inlaid with white or black clays in what was called *Mishima* style. Another important class of tea-ware was a soft pottery with smooth waxen glaze in brown, black, salmon red, or yellow colours, known as Raku ware and introduced by a Corean named Ameya early in the sixteenth century. A seal engraved with the word *Raku* (Happiness) was given to Chojiro, the second generation of the family in 1588, and has been used by his descendants ever since. Raku ware was easily made and required only a low temperature in the baking; it has been manufactured by a large number of potters, professional and amateur, in various parts of Japan.

Among the old factories Takatori was noted for rich, variegated and mahogany glazes of the Seto style ; Karatsu and Hagi for wares of Corean type ; and Shigaraki for rough archaic pottery with blistered and corrugated glaze. A rich brown or slatey grey stoneware, with no glaze at all or only an accidental covering, was made in Bizen from early times : admirably modelled figures and groups have for long been made at Imbe, in this province. A grey stoneware with translucent glaze specked with brown was made at Iwaki in the province of Soma, and was generally decorated with a tethered horse, the princely badge of the province.   Grey ware with fine inlaid white ornament, a development of the Corean *Mishima* style, is peculiar to Yatsushiro ; and the province of Ise is distinguished by the work of a clever amateur of the eighteenth century whose art name is Banko.   He also worked at Yedo copying Raku, Corean, and Kioto wares. His seal was used by Mori Yusetsu, who revived his work in 1830, and who was further noted for the use of interior moulds for his fine stoneware teapots which show outside the finger-prints of the potter.

The Kioto potters worked in every style, but the district of Awata is specially noted for a beautiful pottery with hard greyish white body and translucent glazes varying from grey to cream colour and finely crackled.   In the early part of the seventeenth century this ware was painted in blue or brown under the glaze ; but in the latter part of that period the celebrated potter, whose art name is Ninsei, learnt the secret of enamelling on the glaze from the porcelain makers in Hizen.   He was followed by the Kenzan, Kinkozan, Hozan, Taizan and other families whose descendants in many cases still produce the finely enamelled Awata faïence.   But the most beautiful pottery of this type is the ivory white ware of the province of Satsuma, with its lustrous velvety surface and scarcely perceptible crackle.   This ware, which probably dates from the seventeenth century, was at first undecorated ; enamelled ornaments were sparingly applied in the eighteenth century, but in modern times the quality of the ware has degenerated and the mass of decoration increased.   Indeed a large proportion of the ware is now sent to Tokio, where it is entirely covered with rich enamels and gilding.   There were other and older wares made in the province of Satsuma with glazes of Seto type, shrivelled glazes resembling shark-skin in texture, mottled tortoiseshell glazes, and brown painted designs, but these are little known or appreciated in Europe.

Another kind of pottery, in close imitation of a Chinese ware called by the Japanese Kochi-yaki, was successfully made by Zengoro Hozen, whose art name is Eiraku. This is a stoneware or semi-porcelain with turquoise, green, and purple glazes usually kept apart by the raised outlines of the ornament, but sometimes laid on singly over the entire piece. Eiraku flourished in the first half of the nineteenth century and his family still uses his seal. He worked at Kioto and in the province of Kishiu or Kii.

Marks on Japanese pottery are incised, stamped, or painted. The stamps or seals are by far the most numerous. They usually give the name of the potter or place of manufacture or, more rarely, the name of the Temple or place where the ware was sold. Japanese craftsmen almost always adopt an " art-name," sometimes more than one, and these are the names that chiefly occur in the potter's marks. Thus Zengoro Hozen signed with the name *Eiraku* and also with the seal *Kahin Shiriu* given to him by a princely patron, while Ogata Shinsho, best known by his art name Kenzan, is credited with at least ten pseudonyms. Japanese potters worked singly, and the number of signatures of professional and amateur potters is immense.

Marks containing the words *tei* (house)[1] and *yen* (garden)[2] correspond to the Chinese " hall marks." The following list is a selection of the most important marks arranged geographically. Japanese marks are usually written in Chinese

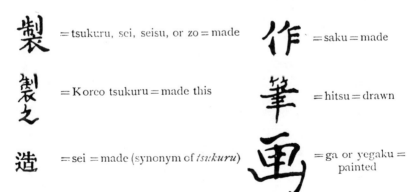

製 = tsukuru, sei, seisu, or zo = made	作 = saku = made
製之 = Korei tsukuru = made this	筆 = hitsu = drawn
造 = sei = made (synonym of *tsukuru*)	畫 = ga or yegaku = painted

script or seal characters, more rarely in the cursive Japanese writing. They commonly end in the word *sei* or *tsukuru* (Ch. *chih*) = made, varied by such words as *saku* = made : *hitsu* (pencil) = drawn : *ga* or *yegaku* = painted. *Tsukuru* followed by the word *Kore* (= this) is read *Kore o tsukuru* = made this. Sometimes the mark ends in, or solely consists of a *Kakihan, i.e.* written seal (see p. 179), a flourish or sign without literary meaning.

Date marks are given in two ways as on Chinese wares: (1) the cyclical system which is identical with the Chinese (p. 129) ; (2) the *nengo* which corresponds with the Chinese *nien hao*, being a period, the name and length of which are determined by the Emperor. The list of *nengo* began in 645 A.D. ; but the following section beginning in 1370 is sufficient for identifying pottery marks. The table of numerals on page 137 will be useful in this connection.

In the columns of Japanese marks the headings in heavy type are the names of provinces. Place-names have been printed in italics, where they might be otherwise confused with the names of potters, which are printed in ordinary type.

JAPANESE DATES (NENGO).

Ken-toku	. . 1370	徳 建
Bun-chū	. . 1372	中 文
Ten-ju	. . 1375	授 天
Kō-wa	. . 1381	和 弘
Gen-chū	. . 1384	中 元
Mei-toku	. . 1393	德 明
Ō-ei	. . . 1394	永 應
Shō-chō	. . 1428	長 正
Ei-kiō	. . . 1429	享 永
Ka-kitsu	. . 1441	吉 嘉
Bun-an	. . 1444	安 文
Hō-toku	. . 1449	德 寶
Kō-toku	. . 1452	德 享
Kō-shō	. . 1455	正 康
Chō-roku	. . 1457	祿 長
Kwan-shō	. 1460	正 寶
Bun-shō	. . 1466	仁 文
Ō-nin	. . 1467	明 應
Bun-mei	. . 1469	亨 文
Chō-kō	. . 1487	德 長
En-toku	. . 1489	應 延
Mei-ō	. . 1492	龜 明
Bun-ki	. . 1501	正 文
Ei-shō	. . 1504	永 永
Dai-ei	. . 1521	祿 大
Kō-roku	. . 1528	文 亨
Tem-bun	. . 1532	天

Kō-ji	. . . 1555	治 弘 永
Ei-roku	. . . 1558	祿 元
Gen-ki	. . . 1570	龜 天
Ten-shō	. . . 1573	正 文 慶
Bun-roku	. . 1592	祿 元
Kei-chō	. . . 1596	長 寛
Gen-na	. . . 1615	和 正 慶
Kwan-ei	. . 1624	永 承
Shō-hō	. . . 1644	保 明
Kei-an	. . . 1648	安 萬 寛
Jō-ō	. . . 1652	應 延
Mei-reki	. . 1655	曆 天 貞
Man-ji	. . . 1658	治 元 享
Kwam-bun	. . 1661	文 寶 正
Em-pō	. . . 1673	寶 正 元
Ten-na	. . . 1681	和 享 寛
Jō-kiō	. . . 1684	祿 元 延
Gen-roku	. . 1688	永 寶
Hō-ei	. . . 1704	德 享 明
Shō-toku	. . 1711	保 元 安
Kiō-hō	. . . 1716	文 寛
Gem-bun	. . 1736	保 延
Kwam-po	. . 1741	享 寶
En-kiō	. . . 1744	延 曆
Kwan-en	. . 1748	和
Hō-reki	. . 1751	永
Mei-wa	. . . 1764	
An-ei	. . . 1772	

JAPANESE DATES (NENGO).

明政和化政保化永延久治應治　天寛享文文天弘嘉安萬文元慶明

Tem-mei	. .	1781
Kwan-sei	. .	1789
Kiō-wa	. . .	1801
Bun-kwa	. .	1804
Bun-sei	. . .	1818
Tem-pō	. . .	1830
Kō-kwa	. . .	1844
Ka-ei	. . .	1848
An-sei	. .	1854
Man-en	. . .	1860
Bun-kiū	. . .	1861
Gen-ji	. . .	1864
Kei-ō	. . .	1865
Mei-ji	. . .	1868

On p. 189 is a complete example of a Japanese mark, including a date, i.e. "Made at Oto-koyama, in Southern Kii, in the first year of Ka-ei" (A.D. 1848). Below are five other examples of date-marks.

Gen-ki nen sei = made in the Gen-ki period (A.D. 1570-73).

Em-po nen sei = made in the Em-po period (A.D. 1673-81).

Mei-ji nen To-yen sei = made by To-yen in the Mei-ji period (A.D. 1868-).

Bun-kwa nen sei = made in the Bun-kwa period (A.D. 1804-1818).

Tai min nen sei = made in the Tai min dynasty i.e. The Great Ming dynasty of the Chinese (A.D. 1368-1644).

MARK.	DESCRIPTION.	MARK.	DESCRIPTION.
	Hizen Shichi ju ni sai Niraku saku = made by Niraku at the age of 72 years c. 1800		**Prov. of Bizen** Various marks used by potters to identify wares fired in the public kilns 17th cent.
			Cho 18th cent.
	Gorohachi. Mark on a copy of old Corean ware, c. 1800. The original Gorohachi worked in the 16th cent.		Ka ichi c. 1680
			Kimura Uji 1780-1830
	Kameyama · 19th cent.		Riku 1780-1830
	Bogasaki, in Nagasaki 1830-43		Totei 19th cent.
	Bo (for Bogasaki)		Dai Nippon Imbe to = Imbe ware of great Japan 19th cent.
	Mikawa for Mikawaji c. 1820		Terami c. 1850
	Shoto c. 1800		K'wa-bo 18th cent.

MARK.	DESCRIPTION.	MARK.	DESCRIPTION.
	Bizen Kiyo-chika 19th cent.		**Tsushima** *Shiga* c. 1820
	Dai Nippon Imbe to (see p.159) and Kimura Kiyochika		**Tosa** *Odo* 19th cent.
	Naoyoshi 18th cent.		Sokan tsukuru = made by Sokan c. 1680
	Ashikage tsukuru = made by Yoshida c. 1840		**Settsu** *Naniwa* (old name of Osaka) c. 1680
	Mori		*Kosobe* and Shichi ju rojin Tai-nen sho = painted by Tainen at the age of 70 years 19th cent.
	Okayama 19th cent.		
	Mushiage		Kikko († 1861) at *Juso*, Osaka 1819 —— (see p. 179)
	Mushiage Makuzu c. 1830		*Sakurai* and no Sato = village of Sakurai c. 1830

MARK.	DESCRIPTION.	MARK.	DESCRIPTION.
松柴 (seal)	**Settsu** Shosai at *Osaka* c. 1860	友吉 喜 (seal)	**Omi** Yuko c. 1850
梅山 勢田	**Omi** Baizan c. 1850 *Seta* 17th cent. onwards	信示	**Shigaraki** ? Uichu. Uichu, potter of *Shigaraki* 17th cent.
蕃	Mompei and Mompeizan c. 1830	方半	
梅林	Bairin at *Beppo* c. 1800	特山 (seal)	Takuzan ; made pottery at *Yedo* (1815-40) with *Shigaraki* clay
湖東 (seal)	**Omi** *Koto* = east of the lake (Biwa). Mark on wares made at *Hikone* 1815-50	縁 (seal) 代 儿	**Higo** Higo *Yatsushiro*
比良	*Hira* c. 1830	源 (seal)	Sogen Gen
芝亭	Zeze Tora. Tora Kichi potter, at *Zeze* c. 1850	東 (seal)	To Kiln marks (see note on Bizen ware, p. 159) on *Yatsushiro* ware 19th cent.

MARK.	DESCRIPTION.	MARK.	DESCRIPTION.
彌	**Higo** Ya late 19th cent.	大樋	**Kaga** *Ohi* 1780 onwards
肥後網田山 紫路	Higo *Amidayama* c. 1797	大樋	Ohi
		卸	Yamamoto c. 1810
	? Kitakoji c. 1840	金府	Kimpu (mark of Mokubei in Kaga) c. 1807
窗	Shofu	安東	**Ise** Anto 1740-1850
軺	**Kaga** Rinzan c. 1800	萬	Banko early 18th cent. onwards
		阿漕	Akogi c. 1850
東邸	Toko at *Rendaiji* c. 1806	左子	Sahei c. 1640

MARK.	DESCRIPTION.	MARK.	DESCRIPTION.
	Ise Banko		**Ise** Yurin, maker of Banko ware 19th cent.
	Banko		Ko-tei = lake house: mark on Banko ware 19th cent.
	Nippon Banko and Date tsukuru = made by Date 19th cent.		*Isawa* c. 1810
	Banko		**Yamato** *Akahada* 18th cent.
	Nippon Yusetsu. Yusetsu was a potter who revived the Banko ware c. 1835		*Akahadayama* (19th cent.)
	Banko Fueki. Fueki was brother of Yusetsu		Bokuhaku (1850-70)
			Issai (Akahada or Hagi) 19th cent.
	Banko		Seto-suke, mark on ware made at Yokka-ichi, in Ise c. 1860
	Bokusai 19th cent.		(also on an older ware made in the province of Echizen c. 1665)

MARK.	DESCRIPTION.	MARK.	DESCRIPTION.
三国	**Echizen** *Mikuni*	日本アヂ三平	**Awaji** Mimpei c. 1830
福井	Fukui c. 1840		*Nippon Awaji* Sampei c. 1880
柳原	**Chikugo** Yanagihawa c. 1840		Rissai (Awaji or Tosa) 19th cent.
當畓	**Suo** Iwakuni (*Tada*) c. 1770	新納軍二郎	Nii-no Gun-jiro 1850
岩國吉向	Iwakuni		**Buzen** Ho and a spiral mark of the potter Hosho at *Agano* c. 1800
十三軒	Kikko (at *Tada*) c. 1835	南 田香	Denko (name of a ware made at *Kataru*) c. 1856
飛金作	Jusan-ken; mark of Kikko	燦燒湊	**Izumi** *Minato* c. 1800, and Minato yaki = Minato ware 19th cent.
	Sado Sa-kin saku = made by Sakin. "Kintaro" ware 1800		

MARK.	DESCRIPTION.	MARK.	DESCRIPTION.
	Izumi		**Kii**
	Sen-shiu Sakai moto Minato yaki Kichi-ye-mon = Original Minato ware of Kichiyemon at *Sakai* in Senshiu (*i.e.* Izumi) 19th cent.		*Otokoyama* near Nishiyama 1847-66
			Nan-ki
	Kwan-kei		Nan-ki. Otokoyama = Otokoyama in Southern Kii
	Iwami		Seinei. A mark said to have been used by Raku Tanniu in Kii c. 1840
	Nag-ami c. 1840		
	Iwao (another mark of the same potter)		Zuishi c. 1790. A ware made at *Meppotani*
	Kii		**Iga**
	Kairakuyen sei = made by Kairakuyen. A name given to Eiraku Hozen by Prince Harunori.		Iga c. 1800 (Two forms of the mark)
	Kairakuyen sei		
	Kairakuyen (in a gourd). The factory was in the Kairakuyen park at Nishiyama and was active from 1828-68		Iga yaki = Iga ware c. 1840
			Totei (at *Marubashiro*) c. 1850

Mark.	Description.	Mark.	Description.
	Nagato *Toyo-ura-yama* c. 1846 (The factory existed from 1716 onwards)		**Harima** *Suma* 1800-50
			Tozan the hill from which the clay was taken for the factory at *Himeji* 1826-
	Totomi *Shidoro* 13th and 19th cent.		**Izumo** Zen and Unzen. A family working at *Fujina* 1750-1860
	Harima *Akashi* (1700-1860)		
	Akashi-ura		Rakuzan at *Matsuye* 1780-1840
	Asagiri Sohei 19th cent. The Asagiri factory dates from 1700-1830		Unyei at *Fujina* c. 1830
			Izumo Wakayama : late 19th cent.
	Wafuken and *Maiko* (1750-1800)		**Chikuzen** Takatori yo = *Takatori* pottery c. 1770
	Hoyen : a mark used by Maisen who followed Wafuken c. 1800		Ka c. 1780
			Yamaka c. 1800 (oven marks see p. 159)

MARK.	DESCRIPTION.	MARK.	DESCRIPTION.
	Chikuzen (Takatori) Ki. c. 1820		*Shido* Shun-min c. 1780
	Taka (for Takatori) 19th cent.		Shun-min
	,,		
	Teiten c. 1850		Min
	Soshichi at *Hakata* 1827		Minzan at *Shido* 1780-1830
	Soshichi		Shinzan c. 1830
	Shun (for Shunzan) in *Suo* c. 1780		Taka (for *Taka matsu*) on "Inari-yama" ware 1740-60
	Sanuki Shun-min Hiraga c. 1780 (Hiraga Gennai took the name Shun-min)		Yashima at *Shido* c. 1800
			Yashima c. 1820

Mark.	Description.	Mark.	Description.
	Sanuki Yashima Rinso tsakuru = Yashima (ware) made by Rinso. 1817		**Owari** Bizan c. 1800. On "Ofuke" ware
			Fuke. Mark on "Ofuke" ware made at Akazu c. 1820
	Yashima		Sobokai 1800
			Shunu c. 1790
	Yohachi 1810-30		Shunzan c. 1770
	San yo = Sanuki Pottery c. 1840		Shuntai c. 1830
	Tamba Naosaku 1835-60		Shunyetsu 19th cent.
	Owari Owari 19th cent.		Shuntan c. 1800

MARK.	DESCRIPTION.	MARK.	DESCRIPTION.
	Owari Makusa c. 1780		**Owari** *Inuyama* 1730 onwards
	Gen (for Gempin) c. 1640		Inuyama (which has the same ideographs as Kenzan) c. 1800
	Gempin on a copy of Gempin ware made c. 1730		
			Yoshitoyo (at *Seto*) c. 1780
	Chozo (at *Tokoname*) c. 1830		Toyohachi (at *Nagoya*)
	Ikko (at *Tokoname*) c. 1850		
	Sobaitei (at *Akazu* or *Kioto*) 18th cent.		Toyosuke
	Masaki (at *Nagoya* and *Tokio*). c. 1820		Toyoraku (or Horaku)
	Bokuko (style of Masaki) 19th cent.		Toyoraku. Four marks on ware made by Toyosuke at the Horaku factory at Nagoya. c. 1820

MARK.	DESCRIPTION.	MARK.	DESCRIPTION.
	Owari Bairaku (on Toyosuke ware) c. 1820		**Yamashiro** Ninsei : in a seal the top of which is like a looped curtain (Maku-in)
	Sasashima (near *Nagoya*) 1750-1870		*Akashi* Mark of Seisuke working with Ninsei c. 1680
	Fuji (marks of the Fujimi family) 1800 onwards		*Seikanji* (Ninsei worked there c. 1670)
	Yamashiro Kuchu : on "Takagamine" ware made by Kuchu or Koho c. 1630 : and Ko in a circle (for Koho)		Onike : on ware made at *Mizoro* early 19th cent.
	Sei (for Ninsei) 17th cent.		Harima : mark of Tsuji Harima 1720-30
	= Kiyoto (mark used by Ninsei)		Tsuji
			Harima
	Ninsei		Fuji (at *Kiyomizu*) c. 1700
	,,		*Awata* (Kioto) 17th cent. onwards
	,,		

MARK.	DESCRIPTION.	MARK.	DESCRIPTION.
	Yamashiro *Iwakura* The Kinkozan family worked at Iwakura, moving to Kioto in 1750, where they used the same marks Iwakurayama Hozan (family) 17th cent. onwards at *Awata* Hozan Taihei (used by Hozan c. 1800) Bu 18th cent. *Gobosatsu* 17th cent. onwards Taizan (at *Awata*) 1760 onwards Giozan 1820-50		**Yamashiro** Kinkozan (at *Iwakura* and *Kioto*). 17th cent. onwards Bizan (at *Awata*) 19th cent. Tanzan (at *Awata*) 1846 —— Kozan c. 1820 *Kiyomizu* (17th cent. onwards) a district of Kioto Kiyo (for Kiyomizu) Kiyomizu Gusai 19th cent. Kanzan (at *Kiyomizu*) 1805 onwards Eisen (at *Kiyomizu*) c. 1760. An amateur potter, who made the first Kioto porcelain

MARK.	DESCRIPTION.	MARK.	DESCRIPTION.
	Yamashiro Roku. Mark of Rokubei I., at *Kiyomizu* (1737-99)		**Yamashiro** Dohachi II. (in a shell)
	Sei in a hexagon. Mark of Rokubei I. and III.		Nin-na and Nin-nami: marks of Dohachi II.
	Rokubei I., and Rokubei III. (1820-85)		Kachutei Dohachi sei = made by Dohachi in the Kachu house
	Sei in a double hexagon. Mark of Rokubei II. 1797-c. 1850		Shuhei : at *Kiyomizu* c. 1810
	Shichibei (1840-60), and Sei in a heptagon : at *Kiyomizu*		Yosobei I. (at *Kiyomizu*) c. 1800 Yosobei II. c. 1830
			Yosobei III. c. 1850
	Dohachi (The first Dohachi dates 1737-93 : Dohachi II. died 1856 : Dohachi III. c. 1840-75 Dohachi IV. 1875-) at *Kiyomizu* Dohachi		Tosetsu : at *Kiyomizu*
			Kitei (at *Kiyomizu*). Four generations dating from 1790

Mark.	Description.	Mark.	Description.
	Yamashiro Kitei : at *Kiyomizu* (Kitei = tortoise house)		**Yamashiro** Tsuyen : at *Kiyomizu* c. 1800
	Ki for Kitei		Ippodo c. 1850 on Suminokura's ware
	Tei on a tortoise : mark of Wake Kitei, c. 1850		*Arashiyama* c. 1830
	A tortoise		Asahitei c. 1840
	Zoroku		Shonsui Gorosuke : at *Gojosaka* 1840-60
	Zoroku (mark of Genyemon at *Kiyomizu*) 1841-		,,
	Otani : mark used by Zoroku		Kinsei c. 1800
	Seifu (at *Kiyomizu*) : three generations dating from c. 1844		Kosai 1840-50

MARK.	DESCRIPTION.	MARK.	DESCRIPTION.

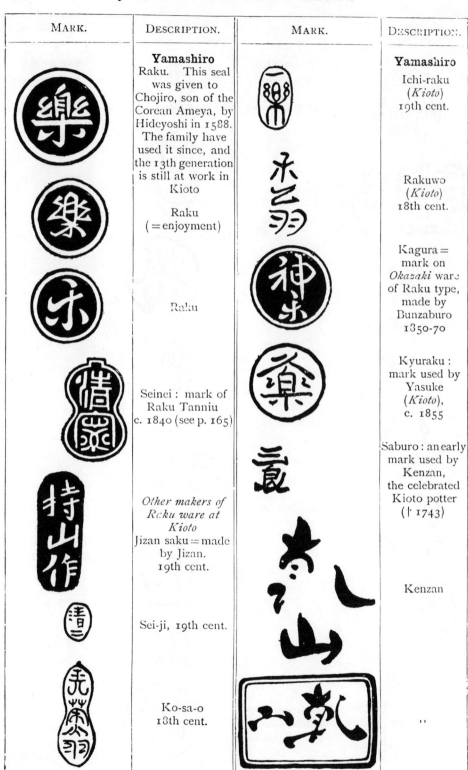

Yamashiro

Raku.   This seal was given to Chojiro, son of the Corean Ameya, by Hideyoshi in 1588. The family have used it since, and the 13th generation is still at work in Kioto

Raku
(=enjoyment)

Raku

Seinei : mark of Raku Tanniu c. 1840 (see p. 165)

Other makers of Raku ware at Kioto
Jizan saku = made by Jizan. 19th cent.

Sei-ji, 19th cent.

Ko-sa-o 18th cent.

Yamashiro

Ichi-raku (*Kioto*) 19th cent.

Rakuwo (*Kioto*) 18th cent.

Kagura = mark on *Okazaki* ware of Raku type, made by Bunzaburo 1850-70

Kyuraku : mark used by Yasuke (*Kioto*), c. 1855

Saburo : an early mark used by Kenzan, the celebrated Kioto potter († 1743)

Kenzan

,,

MARK.	DESCRIPTION.	MARK.	DESCRIPTION.
	Yamashiro Sandai Kenzan = Kenzan of the 3rd generation. early 19th cent.		**Yamashiro** *Omuro* : mark used by Wagen (12th generation of the Zengoro family) c. 1853
			Ouchi-yama Sei en : mark used by Zengoro Wagen
	Mokubei : at *Kiyomizu* (1767-1833) Koki kwan Mokubei tsukuru = made by Mokubei connoisseur of antique pots		Tenkaichi Soshiro : mark of Soshiro, of the 4th generation of the Zengoro family c. 1640
	Asahi : mark on pottery made at *Uji* in 17th cent. and revived in 1852		Marks used by Zenshiro (brother of Wagen) c. 1860 The first reads *Omuro* and the other Toho
	Ryozen c. 1810 (10th generation of the Zengoro family) at Kioto Eiraku : mark of Hozen, 11th generation of the Zengoro family 1825-53 (see p. 165)		*Otowa* 17th cent.
	Kahin Shiriu : mark used by Hozen Hozen		*Otowa* and Ken (for Kentei) c. 1850

MARK.	DESCRIPTION.	MARK.	DESCRIPTION.
玉亭	**Yamashiro** Giyoku-tei (*Kioto*) 18th cent.	鑰軒	**Yamashiro** Kiunken (*Kioto*) 19th cent.
真葛	Makuzu family : 1840 onwards at *Makuzu-ga-hara*, a district of *Kioto*	齊	Sei
花月	Rengetsu : a woman potter 1830-60, and a 2nd generation 1860-80	土圭亥	Shigen late 18th cent.
養山	Koriozan : mark used by Rengetsu	乾し山苛	**Musashi** Kenzan sho = Kenzan wrote it. Kenzan (see p. 174) worked at *Iriya, Tokio* early 19th cent.
富亥	Rantei c. 1865		
（印）	K'wan-riyo (? *Kioto*) late 18th cent.	乾也	Kenya : mark of Miura Kenya in *Asakusa* 1830-c. 1860
朱山	Shuzan c. 1870	乾也	
誠志	Sei shi c. 1872		

Mark.	Description.	Mark.	Description.
	Musashi		**Musashi**
	Kaseizan worked near *Yotsuya, Yedo* c. 1780		Shisei : at *Matsuyama* 19th cent.
	Rakurakuyen : the garden of the Daimio of Owari in *Tokio*, where pottery was made 1804-30. Masaki was in charge for a time		Shoson 19th cent.
	,,		Gosaburo : at *Imado* c. 1840
	Korakuyen : mark of the private kiln of the Prince of Mito, at *Tokio* 1832		
	Sanrakuyen mark of private kiln of the Duke of Tosa, *Tokio* 1848		Sumidagawa : mark used by Kikkutei at *Yedo* 1810
	Kikko, who came to *Yedo* in 1855 (see p. 160)		Tamagawa : probably *Tokio* c. 1850
	Harimoto Sanjiro : at *Imado* 19th cent.		Koren saku == made by Koren : a woman potter of Tokio c. 1878

MARK.	DESCRIPTION.	MARK.	DESCRIPTION.
	Musashi Makuzu Kozan sei (in a gourd) = made by Makuzu Kozan (see p. 176) who moved from Kioto to Yokohama in 1870		**Satsuma** Satsuma : in ordinary and contracted forms
	Makuzu Kozan (in a gourd)		Hoju 1780-1800
	Iwaki Soma. Soma ware was made at *Naka-mura*, 1631 onwards. It is usually decorated with a prancing horse tethered, the device of the Prince of Soma		Hohei 1820
	Yenzan : mark on *Nakamura* ware c. 1850		Hoyei 1820-40
	Kanashige 1850-70		*Tatsumonji* Hoyu c. 1840
	Shoda ? 18th cent. on Soma ware		Hoko 1860
	Komaru 1816- at *Ohorimura*		Seikozan 1830
	Rakuzan 1830 mark used by Komaru		Hayashi (with a leaf usually added). ? Satsuma or Kioto c. 1840

MARK.	DESCRIPTION.	MARK.	DESCRIPTION.
	Satsuma Satsu tsukuru: on *Tachino* ware c. 1830 Tei-ji on netsuke made at ? *Kioto* 19th cent. **Mikawa** Kakitsubata (an iris) and Okunisan (honourable province): marks used on *Kusumura* ware c. 1840 Five examples of Kakihan (hand seals) occasionally used by potters in place of, or accompanying, the ordinary signature. They are mere flourishes made with the brush and do not represent actual characters.		*Miscellaneous* Toshiro : supposed to be the signature of Kato Shirozaemon or Toshiro, the originator of glazed pottery in Japan in the 13th century Sen-ki : mark on *Ohi-machi* ware (see p. 162) 19th cent. Jusan-Ken : mark of Kikko at at Osaka and Yedo (see p. 160) Soyen : mark on Raku ware (*Kioto*) 19th cent. Bunki on Raku ware (*Kioto*) ? 19th cent. Sensuke seizo = made carefully by Sensuke : on *Ota* ware c. 1874 made in the prov. Kii *Ni-Kô* on ware made for sale at the temple of *Niko* near *Tokio*

JAPANESE PORCELAIN

THE pioneer of Japanese porcelain was Gorodayu Go-Shonsui, who spent five years in China learning the art at Ching-tê-chên. Returning to Japan in 1515 he made blue and white porcelain with imported Chinese materials; but as he was unable to find the necessary clay in Japan, his success was only temporary and left nothing behind but the knowledge of painting in blue under a glaze. The requisite materials, however, were discovered in the province of Hizen by a Corean named Risampei, about the year 1605, and forty years later two potters named Tokuemon and Kakiemon, with some help from a Chinese, developed the art of painting in enamel colours. A flourishing industry now sprang up in the village of Arita and its neighbourhood, and much of the ware found its way to Europe on Dutch ships trading with Imari, the sea-port of the Arita district. This "Old Japan" porcelain falls roughly into two classes: (1) a fine white ware with delicate and sparse decoration of floral sprays, birds, and animals in brilliant enamels, blue, manganese-purple, green, and red—commonly called Kakiemon ware; and (2) a heavier, greyer porcelain with crowded ornaments chiefly in dark impure blue, soft Indian red, and gold, obviously made for export, and commonly called Old Imari ware. Two other factories in the province of Hizen were celebrated in the eighteenth and the first half of the nineteenth centuries; the one at Okawaji, under the patronage of the feudal chief of Nabeshima, and the other at Mikawaji, taken under the protection of the chief of Hirado in 1751. The Hirado porcelain was the finest made in Japan; and the best specimens were painted in a pale but pure blue of great delicacy, a favourite subject being boys playing under an ancient pine, the number of boys, seven, five, or three, indicating the quality of the piece.

In 1660 Goto Sajiro, a native of the province of Kaga, set out to discover the secrets of the Arita potters, and from his return in 1664 dates the growth of a flourishing industry at Kutani-mura and its neighbouring villages. Kaga porcelain was chiefly noted for its rich enamels—blue, green, purple, and red— either painted in the Arita style or laid on in broad washes over formal designs pencilled in black. In the nineteenth century a specialty was made of decoration in red and gold, which has come to be regarded as typical of Kaga ware.

The Kioto potters did not turn their attention to porcelain till the end of the eighteenth century. Eisen was the first and he was followed by Mokubei, Rokubei, Eiraku, Dohachi, and a number of other clever potters. The Seto factories, destined to be the most productive in Japan, owe their knowledge of porcelain-making to Kato Tamikichi, who penetrated the secrets of the Arita potters in the first decade of the nineteenth century.

Chinese influence is almost always apparent in Japanese porcelain, and the early wares, if marked at all, usually display a Chinese date,[1] symbol, or mark of commendation. Moreover, the better factories were directly under the patronage of a feudal chief who did not permit the workmen's names to appear on the wares. Thus it is not till the nineteenth century that true potters' marks are common on Japanese porcelain ; and much of the older wares have no mark at all. Marks beginning with the words "*Dai Nippon*" (see p. 186) may be safely regarded as of nineteenth-century date.

[1] Such as the *nienhao* of the Ch'êng Hua (Jap. Seika), Chia Ching (Jap. Ka-sei), Wan Li (Jap. Man-reki), Ch'ien Lung (Jap. Ken-riu) for which see p. 135.

MARK.	DESCRIPTION.	MARK.	DESCRIPTION.
	Bun-mei Kai-k'wa = enlightenment and civilisation : on *Seto* ware c. 1860		On Arita porcelain
	Hô = precious : on Arita porcelain c. 1700		Fuku = happiness (common on Kaga porcelain)
	Hô tei no takara = a gem among precious vessels. on Arita ware 18th cent.		,,
	Kin (gold) : on Okawaji ware 18th cent.		Jiu = long life
	Ka = happiness		,,
	Roku = emolument : on Hirado ware 18th cent.		Doubtful seal mark on Kaga porcelain. early 18th cent.
	? Fu wan chih = made by Fu-wan. on Arita ware c. 1800 Fu wan = ten thousand blessings		Doubtful seal. mark on Kaga ware 17th cent.

MARK.	DESCRIPTION.	MARK.	DESCRIPTION.
	Doubtful seal mark : Arita porcelain ? 18th cent.		Flower in red, and mark of the Dresden collection incised. Arita porcelain 17th cent.
	Sei = made (to order) : on Kaga porcelain 18th cent.		Leaf mark copied from the Chinese
	Ornamental seal mark on Arita porcelain 18th cent.		fungus mark : copied from the Chinese
	Gwan = a trinket. *Kameyama* ware early 19th cent.		
	Seigen = pure trinket. *Seto* ware 19th cent.		Fungus mark
			Hizen
	Fuki cho shun = Riches, honour and eternal spring !		Arita
	Swastika or fylfot symbol : the Chinese wan = ten thousand		Nishina Arita ware 19th cent.
	Five-leaved flower in red on Arita porcelain 17th cent.		

MARK.	DESCRIPTION.	MARK.	DESCRIPTION.
肥前宮 年木庵 喜三製 喜三製 深川製 辻製 信甫造 年木庵 日肥山肥前 肥礫山 古 (seal mark)	**Hizen** Hizen Kuwan Yo Nembokuan Kizo sei = made by Nembokuan Kizo in the Hizen government kiln. Arita 19th cent. Nembokuan Kizo tsukuru = made by Nembokuan Kizo Nichi Hizen yama Fukagawa tsukuru = made by Fukagawa in Hizen yama Arita late 19th cent. Hizen Tsuji tsukuru = made by Tsuji in Hizen. late 19th cent. Hichozan Shimpo tsukuru = made by Hichozan Shimpo. Arita 19th cent. Kozan sho = written by Kozan ? Okawaji 18th cent.	肥前三川内 皿山森力造 平戸 制衣 正 (seal) 藏春亭 三保製 (comb pattern illustration) (seal mark)	**Hizen** Hizen Sarayama. late 19th cent. Mikawaji Mori Chikara tsukuru = made by Mori Chikara at Mikawaji. late 19th cent. Hirato sei = made at Hirato (on Mikawaji ware) Masa-ichi : a netsuke maker : Mikawaji 19th cent. Zôshun tei Sampo sei = made by Sampo at the Zôshun hall Mikawaji c. 1830 Kushide (comb pattern) on the foot rim of Nabeshima ware made at Okawaji 18th and 19th cent. Hako sei = made at Hakodate c. 1850

MARK.	DESCRIPTION.	MARK.	DESCRIPTION.
吳祥瑞造 五良大甫	**Hizen** Gorodayu Go Shonsui tsukuru = made by Gorodayu Go Shonsui. This potter was the originator of Japanese porcelain in the 16th cent.: imitations of his ware are common	椒末又 九谷造 大日本	**Settsu** Sakurai no Sato = the village of Sakurai 19th cent. (see p. 160)
五良大甫所製 倣余祖先祥瑞	Waga sosen Shonsui Gorodayu no tsukuru tokoro ni narau = imitation of ware made by my ancestor Shonsui Gorodayu		**Kaga** *Kutani.* Dai Nippon Kutani zo = made at *Kutani* in Great Japan. 19th cent.
亀山製	Kameyama sei = made at *Kameyama* 1803-46		Tozan no in = seal of Tozan. *Kutani* 19th cent.
姫路製	**Harima** Himeji sei = made at *Himeji* (see p. 166) c. 1826	九谷	*Kutani* Shiozo. late 19th cent.
東山 播陽	*Banyo Higashi yama*	珍玩 道仌	Dosuke chin gwan = precious trinket of Dosuke. Kaga ware 18th cent.

MARK.	DESCRIPTION.	MARK.	DESCRIPTION.
	Yamashiro Kioto		**Yamashiro** Heian toko Rantei seizo = carefully made by Rantei the Kioto potter. early 19th cent.
	Dai Nippon Eiraku tsukuru = made by Eiraku in Great Japan. Mark of Eiraku I. early 19th cent. and Eiraku III. late 19th cent. (see p. 175)		
	Kachu tei Dohachi sei = made by Dohachi in the Kachu house. *Kioto* c. 1840		Rantei sei gwan = pure trinket of Rantei
			Rantei
	Heian toko Rokubei sei = made by Rokubei the Heian potter. Heian is an old name for Kioto. early 19th cent. (see p. 172)		Kisui seizo = made by Kisui. *Kioto* late 19th cent.
	Yaki nushi Sosendo = the potter Sosendo. *Seto* c. 1840		Shimbei tsukuro = made by Shimbei ? *Seto* 19th cent.

MARK.	DESCRIPTION.	MARK.	DESCRIPTION.
	Yamashiro		**Yamashiro**
扒園造	Kiyen tsukuru = made by Kiyen. (incised). *Kioto* 19th cent.	幹山 清製	Kanzan sei sei = carefully made by Kanzan. *Kioto* 19th cent.
大日本 香齋製	Dai Nippon Kosai tsukuru = made by Kosai in Great Japan. *Kioto* c. 1850	幹山 欽裝	Kanzan kin sei = respectfully made by Kanzan
香齋	Kosai	香山造 眞葛窯	Makuzu gama Kozan tsukuru = made by Makuzu Kozan. *Kioto* 1851 ——
大日本 清風造	Dai Nippon Seifu tsukuru = made by Seifu in Great Japan. *Kioto* 19th cent.	眞葛造 不二窯	Fuji gama Makuzu tsukuru = made at the Fuji kiln of *Makuzu*. Makuzu is here the district of Kioto. early 19th cent.
清風	Seifu tsukuru	玉清製 復春軒	Fuku shun ken Giyokusei tsukuru = made by Giyokosei in the Fukushun garden *Kioto* late 19th cent.
周平製 民彤 左平	Ogata Shuhei. *Kioto.* c. 1810	路走貳	= Roki, maker. *Kioto* 19th cent.
	Sahei kore-o-tsukuru = made by Sahei. Mark of Zoroku. *Kioto* 19th cent.		

Mark.	Description.	Mark.	Description.
嘉永元年 南紀男山製	**Kii** Kayei g'wan nen Nanki Otokoyama sei = made at *Otokoyama*, in southern (Kii) in the first year of Kayei (*i.e.* 1848) (see p. 158)	大日本尾張 瀬戸製	**Owari** Dai Nippon Seto sei = made at *Seto* in Great Japan 19th cent.
湖東	**Omi** Koto = east of the lake (*i.e.* lake *Biwa*). early 19th cent. (see p. 161)	加藤勘四郎	Owari
鳴鳳	Meiho : a signature on *Koto* ware		Kato Kanshiro. *Seto* late 19th cent.
湖東 自然庵	Koto Jinenan ji = porcelain of Jinenan of *Koto*	凱	Seal mark on *Seto* ware 19th cent.
名古屋	**Owari** *Nagoya* 19th cent.	川本 枡吉	Kawamoto Masukichi. *Seto* late 19th cent.

MARK.	DESCRIPTION.	MARK.	DESCRIPTION.
	Owari		**Mino**
	Yama-han. *Seto* late 19th cent.	五助製 陶玉園	Togiyokuyen Gosuke sei = made by Gosuke in the Togiyoku garden. 19th cent.
北半製 奇陶軒	Kito ken Kita han sei = made by Kitahan at the Kito (curious pottery) house. *Seto* late 19th cent.		
五陶㞺 昔周園	Seikan yen Goho sei = made by Goho in the Seikan garden. *Seto* late 19th cent.	加籐五輔製　日本美濃國	Nippon Mino no kuni Kato Gosuke sei = made by Kato Gosuke in the province of Mino, Japan
	Mark on ? Kòrakuyen, or Mito, ware made at *Tokio* with *Seto* materials 1832 (see p. 177)		
	A tortoise : on *Seto* ware 19th cent.	大和生	Yamato tsukuru = made at *Yamato* on eggshell porcelain 19th cent.
			Awaji
羊介製 大日本 園製 陶玉	Dai Nippon Hansuke tsukuru = made by Hansuke in Great Japan. *Seto* late 19th cent.	賀集三平　日本淡路	Nippon *Awaji* Kashu Sampei. late 19th cent.
	Mino Togyoku yen sei = made in the Togyoku (jade pottery) garden. *Mino.* 19th cent.		

MARK.	DESCRIPTION.	MARK.	DESCRIPTION.
瓢池園画　日本東京　於香蘭社　西山製　七寶會社	Nippon Tok:o Hyochiyen gua = painted at the Hyochi garden *Tokio.* On Arita ware painted at Tokio. 19th cent.	ニッポン東京　錦窰舍精製	Nippon Tokio Kinyosha sei sei = carefully made by the Kinyo Company at *Tokio* in Japan. late 19th cent.
	Koransha ni oite Seizan sei = made by Seizan of the Koransha (company). *Arita* late 19th cent.		
	Shippo Kwaisha : mark of the Shippo Company *Owari* late 19th cent.		

INDEX OF NAMES

INDEX OF INITIALS

INDEX OF MARKS OTHER THAN NAMES AND INITIALS

INDEX OF ORIENTAL MARKS
AND NAMES

INDEX OF ADDITIONAL NAMES

INDEX OF ADDITIONAL INITIALS

INDEX OF ADDITIONAL MARKS OTHER THAN NAMES AND INITIALS

INDEX OF ADDITIONAL ORIENTAL MARKS